Eyewitness to History

Eyewitness to History

William Bleasdell Cameron
Frontier Journalist

Edited by R. H. Macdonald

Western Producer Prairie Books
Saskatoon, Saskatchewan

Printed and bound in Canada by
Modern Press
Saskatoon, Saskatchewan

Cover design by John Luckhurst/GDL
Cover photograph courtesy Saskatchewan Archives Board, R-B3938

Western Producer Prairie Book publications are produced and manufactured
in the middle of Western Canada by a unique publishing venture owned by a
group of prairie farmers who are members of Saskatchewan Wheat Pool.
From the first book published in 1954, a reprint of a serial originally carried
in the weekly newspaper, *The Western Producer*, to the book before you now,
the tradition of providing enjoyable and informative reading for all Canadians
is continued.

The publisher acknowledges the support received for this publication from the
Canada Council.

Canadian Cataloguing in Publication Data

Cameron, William Bleasdell, 1862-1951.
    Eyewitness to history

Includes index.
ISBN 0-88833-141-X

1. Northwest, Canadian — History — 1870-1905 —
Addresses, essays, lectures.* 2. Cameron, William
Bleasdell, 1862-1951. I. Macdonald, R. H., 1915-
II. Title.
FC3217.C35 1985   971.2'02   C85-091318-7
F1060.9.C35 1985

C,3

48,538

To the Cree who, in their mysterious manner, preserved the life of N'Chawamis—their Little Brother—who in turn would capture them and their era in authentic, vivid detail.

Contents

Preface

William Bleasdell Cameron was no stranger to us in the offices of *The Western Producer*. He was not a talkative man but his situation toward the end of his life placed him in a position of being obliged to say a few words to us from time to time. He was usually short of funds and at the same time uncertain of his next forwarding address. Therefore when he delivered his manuscripts we had to issue a cheque there and then; while he waited we chatted. Seldom did we have the opportunity to spend a few moments with a more interesting person.

Following his death, and with renewed interest in the history of the West inspired by jubilees and local history books, we decided to track down the heirs to Cameron's copyrights with a view to bringing his book *The War Trail of Big Bear* back into print. As it happened, we did not have the opportunity to reprint the book but we did discover the treasure of Vancouver Island. It was in a trunk shaped for all the world like an ancient sea captain's chest. There were no pearls nor gold but, to us, something much more valuable—the papers of W. B. Cameron.

The sequence of events which led to this discovery began in 1970 when we asked the late Ken Liddell if he had ever met relatives of William Bleasdell Cameron in his wide-ranging search for material for his Calgary *Herald* column. A year or so later, Liddell learned there were relatives in Montreal and in a small town in British Columbia, but he did not know which one. This clue eventually led us to Owen Cameron and his wife Jessie in Squamish, discovered through a call to a number picked on a hunch from the back section of the Vancouver telephone directory. From there we were referred to Mrs. D. W. (Elsie) Cameron, on Vancouver Island.

It was in Mrs. Elsie Cameron's home overlooking the Straight of Georgia that Cameron's steamer trunk was produced and opened for the first time since his death in 1951. It was packed with manuscripts, photographs, scrapbooks, letters, and books, just as her late husband Douglas had placed them following his father's funeral at Meadow Lake, Sask., more than twenty years before. The idea for a book such as this one began to take shape.

Thus began a pleasant association with Mrs. Elsie Cameron and with Mrs. Jessie Cameron of Squamish (who also had memorabilia), the Cameron daughters-in-law, and eventually with Mrs. Elaine Morton, one of the Cameron grandchildren chosen by the others to represent them in anything having to do with copyright of their grandfather's material to which they had fallen heir. Delayed for various reasons in the interim, it has taken more than fourteen years to produce this volume.

As Cameron's writings spanned from the Victorian era to the jet age so did the style, treatment, spelling, and usage vary widely. Little attempt has been made to alter these and so the excerpts appear today much as they did ninety years ago, save for their new dress in modern type face and some minor alterations.

Fiction, it has been said, does not travel well between one era and another, but some of Cameron's stories (usually based on fact) are included here without apology because the atmosphere and background he created are authentic and transport the reader, as if by magic carpet, firmly to the North-West Territories of the last century. Certain terms may offend—"savage," "young bucks," and "halfbreed," for instance—but these reflect the times rather than any negative attitude of Cameron towards his subjects. He was sympathetic and respectful to native people and, in many ways, his understanding was much more liberal than many ideas held today.

During the search for Cameron's heirs, it was found that little had been published about the man and his writings. Because he was an eyewitness during an important era in western Canadian history, and an honest reporter, journalist, and able writer, it was felt that something more than a brief *Who's Who* should be presented here. The result is a comprehensive biography which appears as an Introduction to this book.

A number of institutions and persons contributed greatly to the preparation of this work. Public libraries of help include those in Saskatoon, Regina, Calgary, Edmonton, Lethbridge, Vancouver, Victoria, Winnipeg, and Toronto, as well as the National Library of Canada in Ottawa. Also consulted were the Saskatchewan Archives Offices in Saskatoon and Regina, the Provincial Archives of Alberta, British Columbia, Manitoba, and Ontario, and the Hudson's Bay Company Archives in Winnipeg. Valuable assistance came from the Glenbow-Alberta Institute, Calgary; Archives of the Canadian Rockies, Banff; Royal Canadian Mounted Police Museum, Regina; Western Development Museum Library, Saskatoon; Vital Statistics Branch, Department of Health, Regina; Fort Macleod Museum, Fort Macleod; Saskatchewan Legislative Library, Regina; and Trafalgar Castle School, Whitby, Ontario. American institutions extending friendly assistance were: Manuscript Division, Library of Congress, Washington, D.C.; Wilson Library, Western Washington State College, Bellingham, Wash.; Washington State Historical Society, Tacoma; Minnesota Historical Society, St. Paul; and Pacific Northwest Bibliographic Center, Seattle.

Of service were the files of Saskatoon *Star-Phoenix*, Regina *Leader-Post*, Winnipeg *Free Press*, North Battleford *News-Optimist*, Meadow Lake *Advance*, Edmonton *Journal*, Calgary *Herald*, Calgary *Albertan*, Vancouver *Sun*, and Vancouver *Daily Province*, as well as many major newspapers that reviewed books in the 1920s. Periodicals of help include *The Beaver*, *The Western Producer*, *Country Guide*, *Farm and Ranch Review*, and *Scarlet and Gold*. Publishers mentioned in connection with reprinted articles and excerpts appearing in this volume were generous with their permissions.

The full co-operation of Elsie Cameron, Jessie Cameron and Elaine Morton is gratefully acknowledged as is that of Cameron's grandchildren: Gail Noreen, Glen Douglas, Leslie Anne, children of the late Douglas, and of Elsie Cameron; William Ross, James Owen, Gordon Muir, Elaine Marie, children of the late Owen, and of Jessie Cameron, who gave full permission to reproduce Cameron writings, papers, documents, and books.

In addition to the aforementioned institutions, help was given by: Mrs. Betty Savich, Weston, Ontario; Bruce Peel, former librarian of the University of Alberta, Edmonton; H. H. Tibbetts, Fort Frances, Ontario; E. L. Meers, Red Deer, Alberta; L. McIntosh, Meadow Lake *Progress*; Charles Woodman, Meadow Lake; Bert Jackson, New Westminster, British Columbia; and Doris Macdonald whose valuable assistance contributed much to the book.

Finally the editor thanks Hugh A. Dempsey, curator, Glenbow Alberta Institute. Dr. Dempsey read the entire manuscript making valuable suggestions for the good of the whole project.

To these, and many unmentioned, the editor owes his gratitude.

Introduction

It is fortunate for western Canada that William Bleasdell Cameron, the writer of these stories, appeared on the scene when he did. Had he not, an important part of its social history would now be much less distinct than it is. Whatever he observed, he captured in unforgettable word pictures for the entertainment of his contemporaries and the enlightenment of posterity.

Cameron, commonly called Bleasdell Cameron, was born in Trenton, Ontario, on July 26, 1862, the son of John Cameron and Agnes Emma (Bleasdell) Cameron. John, who was involved in the lumbering industry, died when Cameron was yet a boy. His mother was the daughter of a well known clergyman, W. M. Bleasdell, MA, DCL, Canon of St. George's Anglican Church, Trenton.[1]

Cameron remembered little of his father but he revered his mother and grandfather. In later years he spoke of the stone vicarage surrounded by lawns and shade trees. It was here in boyish play that he met with a serious accident, losing an eye; family lore says the game was cowboys and Indians, and that an arrow put out the eye.

He also had an early introduction to books and reading. Canon Bleasdell recognized his curiosity and encouraged him to select and read books from a generous library, presenting him with copies to keep on his own shelves. From this beginning he developed into an avid reader.

Cameron entered public school in Trenton in 1868 and high school in 1876. Upon graduating, he began a career as an apprentice in a drug store operated by a member of the Bleasdell family. But adventure called and he headed west. He left Trenton in July 1881 and, taking the railway through Chicago and St. Paul, he travelled northward by boat to Winnipeg.

Truly in search of adventure, he turned his back on city life and became employed as a helper on a Red River cart brigade carrying supplies to Battleford, then the capital of the North-West Territories. There he met Bob Young, local manager for merchant Sandy Macdonald,[2] who offered him a job as assistant manager and the opportunity to learn how to trade with the Cree Indians. He soon learned to speak their language and began close observation of their manners and customs.

Cameron bought land in Battleford and in 1883 he sold it at a profit. With two hundred dollars in his pocket, he headed farther west in search of adventure. Years later he said, "The population of Battleford was becoming too white, so I moved on."

The Canadian Pacific Railway by now had crossed the prairie two hundred miles south, and Battleford merchants were eager to establish a new railhead for their supplies. They made a deal with Cameron to break a new trail southward through Eagle Hills, across the South Saskatchewan River and on to the new station of Swift Current. Hiring Chief Poundmaker's son as a guide, he left Battleford at the head of a train of a hundred Red River carts to carve a trail over prairie sod to a detached boxcar on a siding which marked the future site of Swift Current. With good navigation they struck the railway only a few hundred yards from the marker. Cameron was then only twenty-one years old—but a trailblazer nevertheless.

Turning west with his team of horses and wagon, he stopped at Medicine Hat to work as a pile driver on the CPR bridge across the South Saskatchewan River. This job done, he continued west through Blackfoot country ("there's nothing subdued about them") to a point east of Calgary where future Alberta cabinet minister W. H. Cushing had a contract to construct railway grades.

Cameron's next job was as a cowboy, riding the range for the Cochrane Ranch Company. From there he entered the Rocky Mountains to join the labourers building the CPR line through the rugged passes.

In 1884 he turned to Indian trading. At Pincher Creek he outfitted himself and after laying in supplies—eleven horses, blankets, traps, ammunition, bacon, tea, fabrics, and other attractive items—he turned north-east toward Battleford and the Crees. As an independent trader, having mastered the Cree language and knowledge of their habits, he soon gained their respect. As his reputation grew among them, and perhaps because he was young, short and slim, they gave him the name N-Chawamis or My Little Brother. More than a name, it would become a talisman, averting evil in troubled times ahead.

In April 1884, Cameron set up business at Frog Lake, a promising location where Woodland Crees had selected their reserves. The Plains Crees under Chief Big Bear also camped at Frog Lake, having refused to select a reserve of their own. The Hudson's Bay Company had a post at Frog Lake as did another independent trader, George Dill. Soon after his arrival, Cameron and Dill became partners for a few months, until it became clear there was trade enough to support only one person. Accordingly, Cameron sold out and left for Battleford, eventually joining the venerable Hudson's Bay Company. In 1885, he was sent back to Frog Lake as a clerk under the benign supervision of trader James K. Simpson. Cameron soon re-established close relations with the Cree community, sharing meals on occasion with old Chief Big Bear whom he admired as man and leader. To the chief and most of his tribe, Cameron was still My Little Brother.

During this period, disturbing rumours continued to circulate. Relations between the Metis in the Batoche-Duck Lake area and the Canadian government in Ottawa were troubled. The Metis had sent a delegation to Montana, inviting Louis Riel to return from exile. He accepted the invitation and returned to Canada to become their leader, with headquarters in Batoche and on March 19, 1885, proclaimed a provisional government, just as he had done at the Red River colony in 1869. Rumour of trouble turned to fact on March 26, when a force of North-West Mounted Police and Prince Albert Volunteers, seeking to establish government authority, were met by a Metis and Indian force at Duck Lake. When the fight was over, the government force retired with ten dead and thirteen wounded, while Metis held the field, with casualties of five dead and one wounded.

The news that the NWMP had suffered its first defeat spread over the plains like a prairie fire in a strong wind. At Frog Lake it was greeted with concern among some Indians and whites, but with glee and anticipation by the malcontents in Big Bear's band. On April 2, 1885, Big Bear's younger warriors sacked the village of Frog Lake and killed the white residents. Nine whites fell and two of their women were taken prisoner. Cameron, the Little Brother, escaped harm with the aid of Indian friends but became a prisoner in Big Bear's camp. There he remained for two months, watched closely and threatened with death several times and moved from camp to camp, as the Indians evaded the government military force sent to capture them.

Cameron eventually escaped, then immediately volunteered and was accepted as guide and scout with General Strange's Alberta Field Force now in hot pursuit of the rebellious Crees.

Following the government victory at Batoche on May 12, 1885, and Riel's surrender three days later, peace was restored and Cameron became involved in the subsequent trials. He gave eyewitness evidence on the Frog Lake massacre and attempted to ameliorate the sentence of his old friend Big Bear. The chief was sentenced to three years in Stony Mountain penitentiary; others were hanged.

Upon being honourably discharged from his service with the Dominion forces, Cameron returned to eastern Canada for a tearful but happy reunion with his mother and three sisters, now living in Toronto. In 1886 he wrote and passed civil service examinations, being posted back west to Regina where he was listed variously on the staff of the land department in that city and the Indian Agency at Duck Lake. His mother joined him at Duck Lake for a time, later leaving for Battleford to join the administration of a residential school for Indians.

It appears that the next five years in civilization left Cameron eager to move to the frontier for by 1891 he was listed as an employee of the HBC at Fort Alexander, located on the east shore of Lake Winnipeg at the mouth of the Winnipeg River. It is here that he first became interested in writing. He began freelancing some time in 1891 and within two or three years he was selling to quality journals such as *Waverley Magazine, Harper's Weekly,* and *Toronto Saturday Night.* The latter magazine held a contest and published Cameron's first prize-winning article, "A Reconnaissance of Fort Ellice," in its Christmas issue of 1895. His was judged the best out of a hundred and forty manuscripts entered in the contest and apparently this was enough to move him toward big time writing. During this period at Fort Alexander he also began correspondence with Owen Wister, the famous author of cowboy stories, a relationship that would last until the latter's death in 1938.

In 1896 Cameron joined the staff of the *News Tribune* in the city of Duluth, Minnesota, and in a short time was promoted to the position of telegraph editor and editorial writer. When he left that job a year later, he carried with him a recommendation stating that he was "a graceful writer" and they were sorry to see him leave.[3] He next emerged in St. Paul on the staff of the recently formed *Western Field and Stream.* This magazine featured his photo on its December 1896 editorial page as a prize-winning writer who had joined the staff and would be contributing in future.

The job seemed ideally suited to Cameron who was in search of adventure on the frontier, as the work took him out to the American West looking for copy and photographs. On one such trip to Montana he met a cowboy artist, admired his work, and signed him up to deliver a series of Indian and western scenes to *Western Field and Stream* for publication. Such exposure would do much for the artist, spreading his name far beyond the borders of his state. The name: C. M. "Charley" Russell.

Two years after joining the staff of *Western Field and Stream*, there were fundamental changes in the publication. Reflecting its expanding national and international subscription list, it dropped *"Western"* from its title and now was simply *Field and Stream*. The masthead of the April 1898 issue indicated that "Wm. Bleasdell Cameron" was the editor, but the address had changed from St. Paul to New York.

The sport and outdoor magazine was obviously developing its personality and adding to its circulation with each issue. Cameron was rising in responsibility each year; later he told a friend that it was he who insisted the journal be moved to New York, close to the developing news agency people, the advertisers, and subscription agency headquarters.

Cameron threw all this up later in August, 1898, and disappeared from the scene almost without a trace. A private person, he was not given to explaining himself to his family, but on July 1, 1899 he did describe his move in a letter to his friend Wister.

"I have been here [Toronto] . . . ever since," he said, "trying to write myself into immortality. I fear that when the Lord distributed divine afflatus round, He did not allow sufficient of it to fall upon me to do any good. However I am working along cheerfully." Despite meagre returns, he commented, "I like the work and . . . it brings me a satisfaction which no success in any other line of work could afford me. I think more of a dollar earned by my own independent effort in this way than I should of five received as wages from other people."[4]

Thus Cameron joined the legions of aspiring writers prepared to starve in a garret for their art. Shortage of funds time and time again prevented him from joining in family events, such as the weddings of his beloved sisters.[5] Freelancing was not a successful venture and, although he sold a number of articles toward the end of the century, he could not have made enough money to carry him above subsistence level.

He did, however, write one manuscript that would play a key role in establishing him as a serious writer. As he explained in a letter to his friend Wister in 1898: "I wrote a book last winter—a narrative of the 'Big Bear' troubles of 1885 on the Saskatchewan [River]. It is now in London, but I do not know when, if ever, it will be published." He would have to wait for well over a quarter of a century to see it in print.

In 1899 Cameron returned to the West, never again to reside in eastern Canada for any length of time. The Wister letters reveal in a sketchy way that he had turned away from writing full time to other ventures. Included in these was a period spent in the Rainy Lake-Fort Frances district of western Ontario in the lumber business. Other letters in the Cameron papers revealed the presence of a young lady in his life. From her letters to him it is established that she was living in a railway hotel owned by an uncle who catered to the lumber trade and to main line railway passengers during their brief stops.

Her name was Mary Maude Atkins and she was an unlikely match for him, he being forty years old, she twenty-seven. According to family lore Miss Atkins had had an unfortunate love affair at her home in Napanee, Ontario. Following her public and high school terms her parents sent her to Whitby College (now Trafalgar Castle School) in Whitby, a finishing school for young ladies. One way or another she met a young man and they fell in love. It was an ill-starred romance, however, she being Protestant and he Catholic. The marriage was forbidden so she moved to Fort Frances to help out in the dining room of the railway hotel. She was unhappy with her prospects.

Disparate though their ages were, they married in 1902. Other letters suggest that Cameron continued to move about, taking his wife as far west as Spokane, Washington, where he worked for a newspaper. Shortly afterwards, his wife returned to Fort Frances to be joined by him later. A son was born to the couple in 1904. He was named Owen, after Owen Wister whose articles on cowboys in the American West had been recently gathered and published as a book, *The Virginian*, and was the talk of the nation.

A land rush and wheat boom was taking place in the Canadian prairies so Cameron moved to Vermilion, Alberta, in 1906 where he took land, opened a commercial printing business, and established a weekly newspaper, *The Signal*. He took an active part in community affairs, becoming secretary of the Board of Trade in 1905, a member of town council in 1907-08, and a notary public. It was here in 1908 that Cameron's second and last child, Douglas, was born. According to *Who's Who in Western Canada* (1911), Cameron was a Mason and his hobbies were hunting, camping, fishing, and riding.

In 1910 he sold *The Signal* and moved to the new and booming CPR irrigation centre of Bassano, Alberta, where he established

The Bassano News. Soon afterwards he sold out to Leonard D. Nesbitt, a Calgary *Herald* reporter, and J. R. Sharp of the Calgary *Albertan.*[5]

Cameron then went to Calgary to join the real estate boom. According to Nesbitt he was "not too successful." About this time, according to an undated newspaper clipping in Cameron's papers, there is mention of him becoming assistant manager of the Winnipeg Exhibition. By 1917 he was in North Vancouver, B.C., and during this period he was listed in Henderson's Directory variously as traveller, salesman, and journalist. His name then disappeared while those of his wife and sons remained. It is known that at one time Cameron represented a drug company and publishers, possibly selling subscriptions.

Nineteen twenty-five was a watershed year in Cameron's writing career. He had written and had done some editing for *Scarlet and Gold Annual,* published by the Royal North-West Mounted Police Veterans Association, Vancouver, when he was invited by the Historic Sites and Monuments Board of Canada to officiate at the unveiling of a cairn marking the site of the Frog Lake massacre. This he did on June 9, 1925.

Among others attending the ceremony was Howard A. Kennedy, an influential writer and member of the Canadian Authors' Association. He had been a reporter for the Montreal *Daily Witness* during the 1885 rebellion and later made a name for himself as editor of the London *Times* weekly supplement in England. Cameron had his "Big Bear" manuscript with him and he let Kennedy have it to read.

Reaction was immediate—and favourable. Kennedy took the manuscript with him to a Canadian Authors' Association meeting in Winnipeg where he told the assembly that "it was immense—I did not know of any book published in or on Canada in the last twenty years that had so thrilled me."[6] The manuscript was accepted and published as *The War Trail of Big Bear* by Duckworth and Company in Britain and the Ryerson Press in Canada.

It was an immediate hit and accorded full treatment in book review pages in Montreal, Toronto, Winnipeg, Calgary, Saskatoon, Edmonton, Vancouver, and in London, England, as well as in the United States by the Washington Historical Quarterly.[7]

The first printing of 2,500 copies was sold out in little over three months. A second printing of 1,500 sold out in a short time as well. Then Cameron seemed to get a further break when an American publisher undertook to give his book exposure in the lucrative United States market. But Cameron's luck did not hold. The deal was made with Small, Maynard and Company of Boston who were to receive flat, unbound pages from the British printer to bind and sell in the United States. Sadly for Cameron, the American company went broke as the shipment of pages was in mid-Atlantic and they were auctioned upon arrival for whatever they would bring in order to pay the shipping charges against them. When Cameron learned of the calamity, he travelled to New York to salvage what he could. Unfortunately, he had neither the time nor money to redirect the pages to another publisher. They were sold to a jobber and later came out as a book, but Cameron got not a penny from the transaction.

In spite of this setback, Cameron had achieved his life's ambition: he was now a published author and he revelled in it. He toured the country, lecturing, promoting book sales, and giving interviews to the press. Wherever he went his arrival became a newsworthy event. Once again his articles found easy publication and readers appeared eager to read his graphic and authentic descriptions of Indians and life in the North-West Territories in the 1880s.

During this time the Camerons finally dropped all pretences of living together. Cameron and his wife Mary agreed to separate without formal negotiations. At this distance and with the sparsity of information it is difficult to speculate about their reasons. Cameron did confide his side of the case to his son Douglas when he said the parting was "for good and sufficient reason" and that he could never write in the prevailing atmosphere of his home.[8] He referred to his lack of success at moneymaking however, and it is not difficult to imagine Mrs. Cameron's feeling of insecurity engendered by the numerous moves from one place to another which she had experienced during married life. From that point on much, if not all, of the responsibility of the home in North Vancouver fell on the shoulders of the youngest son, Douglas, and did so completely after the Second World War when Mrs. Cameron moved to Montreal and lived with his family until shortly before her death.[9]

The four years that followed the appearance of *The War Trail of Big Bear* were the best of Cameron's life. He was an established author, acclaimed by press and public, and recognized wherever he went. He began producing articles; it was a rebirth, once again editors would take anything he wrote. The CPR paid him a retainer to produce one article per month for its railway publication. For the next three years he toured western Canada promoting the sale of his book and lecturing. Wherever he went he would be asked for copies of his work and he calculated later that he had sold possibly one thousand copies in this manner.

Entertainment was assured at a Bleasdell Cameron lecture. He was well received in the larger cities but he did not confine his attention to them. In two years, Cameron lectured in well over a hundred small towns in Alberta and Saskatchewan. The arrangement in those days was for a silver collection to be taken; this was split between the sponsor and speaker. According to newspaper reports, his audiences got what they paid for. His main theme was the Big Bear experience but he was showman enough to include demonstrations of Indian sign language, war dances and chants in Cree, the lighting of campfires with flint and steel, and lantern slides of some of the main characters of the 1885 uprising.

Cameron's next book arose from a chance encounter during his travels. At Duck Lake, Saskatchewan, he met John Henry Moberly, a retired Hudson's Bay Co. factor who had kept a detailed diary of his experiences in the fur trade long before serious settlement began in the West. They collaborated on a book based on this diary and from accounts related to Cameron by either Moberly or the Indians themselves. What emerged was the classic book *When Fur Was King*. The body of the work comprises the narrative diary, edited by Cameron, and following that, Cameron's account of Indian conflicts based on early accounts handed down in the native oral history. This valuable volume, rescued from oblivion by Cameron, was published in 1929 by J. M. Dent and Sons, with the two collaborators splitting the royalties.

A few years later, following the death of Sir Cecil Denny, the estate of this former member of the original North-West Mounted Police engaged Cameron to edit his writings. This he did on and off over a period of three years for a fee of $400[10] and in 1939 the book was published by J. M. Dent and Sons, Toronto, under the title *The Law Marches West*.

Meanwhile, Cameron did not enjoy public acclaim for long. The Depression of the 1930s removed all markets from the writer in one stroke. He could sell little or nothing for almost ten years.

During this period he fell back on the profession for which he had trained as a youth and had occasionally followed in his Indian trading days—pharmacy. He found that by paying a fee of fifty dollars he could take out a licence to practise in Alberta. There is mention of a number of towns in which he set up for business or lived in temporarily—Harrisburg, Bonnyville, Derwent, Elk Point—but it is known for certain that he had drug stores at Athabasca Landing and Lac la Biche, Alberta.[11]

During his career, Cameron seemed impelled to attach himself to those who achieved the success that evaded him. In 1938, when death removed his most regular correspondent, Owen Wister, it was not long before he began exchanging letters with another. This time it was not a sophisticated American celebrity—whose letters came encrusted with return addresses such as the Harvard Club, Rittenhouse Club, Longhouse, and Bryn Mawr, Pennsylvania—but R. Ross Annett of Consort, Alberta, about one hundred and fifty miles east of Red Deer.

Annett had also been an aspiring writer with New York experience. Thirty-three years younger than Cameron, he moved to Alberta in 1930 when the Depression set in and short story markets dried up. To support his wife and family of growing boys he became principal of Consort Consolidated School, writing during holidays. In time he realized the ambition of all contemporary freelance writers when in 1937 *Saturday Evening Post* accepted a folksy story "It's Gotta Rain Sometime." This grew into a series that became a household favourite and a glimmer of light entertainment for thousands of readers amidst the economic gloom of the Depression. It became known after its two main characters as the "Babe and Little Joe" series.

In 1945, at the request of the Canadian Broadcasting Corporation, Annett also created a radio series for the noon program "Prairie Farm Broadcast." It was called "The Jacksons and Their Neighbours," a daily episode of topical interest to a rural audience. It, too, became required listening in thousands of western households but after a year Annett asked CBC to find another writer to continue it, as it interfered with his own creative work.[12] Then *Saturday Evening Post* agreed to take four "Babe" stories plus four others at $12,000 per year, a lucrative but demanding commitment, leaving little time for other work. In addition, the Walt Disney organization dickered with Annett for film rights to the "Babe" series, although nothing came of it.

Poor Cameron! He did manage to pick as friends, writers who were enjoying fabulous success compared to his occasional sales and meagre returns. First Wister, then Annett! Despite the disparity of their earnings, the exchange was not only of higher frequency than that with Wister, it appears to have been mutually beneficial. They discussed work in progress, praised and criticized each other's writing, toyed with collaboration. Annett paid Cameron as a consultant on one story involving historic background; Cameron put Annett in touch with his son Douglas whose Montreal firm had for him a promotional piece to do. Annett allowed Cameron to live vicariously a family life much more successful than his own as he described the triumphs and tragedies that visited his household in Consort over the ten odd years before Cameron's demise.[13]

As the Depression lifted, Cameron left the drug business in the Alberta hinterland and returned to Vancouver. He had written little or nothing as markets shrank or disappeared altogether. Much to his dismay, when he picked up his writing once more he found the market entirely different from the one he had known. The needs were different, the journals had changed character, and most discouraging of all, the editors and staff were now unknown to him and he to them.[14] As he said to a friend, the new mood was such that one had to write "like Bob Hope" to sell. Still, he dramatized his Big Bear book for the CBC and managed to pick up some old and some new markets including *The Beaver*, *The Western Producer*, and *The Country Guide*. Other sales were made through Millers Services, Toronto.

One would have thought that the ideal arrangement dropped into Cameron's lap when, in 1943, Commissioner S. T. Wood gave him the job as curator of the RCMP museum at Regina. But once again he remained only a short time, leaving for British Columbia in 1944. He had not been able to do any writing as museum work intruded, he told the Regina *Leader-Post*, and so he was going to establish a farm on Vancouver Island and raise mink, which he expected would give him ample spare time for writing.[15]

The experience on the farm, two acres north of Parksville, was disastrous. He had been ignorant of the demands the mercurial dispositions of the furry beasts would make on his time, and the seemingly unending business problems that arose to keep him away from his typewriter.

During the Second World War he lived in New Westminster, Parksville, and Edmonton. While in the latter city he offered his services to an army recruiting officer who recognized him. This gave the press a bright story to play up for a day or so. But in his letters to family and friends he began to refer increasingly to the fact that it was taking him longer to write his articles. His financial situation was relieved somewhat when he applied for a war veteran's allowance on the strength of his service during the rebellion and was granted $30 per month from 1945 onwards. It was not enough to live on, but it helped. Later he applied for a married veteran's allowance but was rejected as he did not live with his wife (who had by then moved to Montreal).

A cluster of extraneous events happened to Cameron in the 1940s. J. K. Cornwall approached him to write Cornwall's biography, living with them in their large house in Victoria; a counter business offer was made by Cameron but nothing came of it. Cameron also offered his services as history consultant to Cecil B. deMille for the movie "North-West Mounted Police," but here again to no avail.

When I met him in Saskatoon, Cameron gave the impression of a man on the run from doctors and nurses of the Department of Veterans' Affairs hospital, who were constantly trying to confine him to bed to build him up against fatigue, pneumonia, and a heart murmur that beset him at intervals. He was a hard man to tie down but he was eighty-eight years old then and age had begun to tell. Even with an editor's open invitation to "send us all the stuff you can—we'll publish it," he seemed unable to take full advantage of the opportunity.[16]

In 1947, at the invitation of Everett Baker, a Saskatchewan Wheat Pool field man who was as much interested in history as he was in grain, Cameron left British Columbia and retraced the Frog Lake and Alberta Field Force route for the camera and for the record. The Pool paid the expenses. A number of others accompanied Baker and Cameron, including Saskatoon *Star Phoenix* reporter Reg Taylor, who wrote a series of stories on the event.[17]

Cameron had never been happy with the title of the Big Bear book, which seemed to place responsibility for the massacre at Frog Lake wrongly on the shoulders of the old chief himself. Over the years, there were others who were interested in the book besides the author. Norman Luxton, founder of a museum in Banff, Alberta, and a long time friend of Cameron's, took an interest in its revival and made a number of suggestions.[18] Thus encouraged, Cameron launched on what was to be the last big project of his life.

After several false starts, but with Luxton involved one way or another, Cameron got his wish—his book would be reissued. Arrangements were made with Ken Coppock, publisher of *The Canadian Cattlemen*, to bring out a revised edition under a more acceptable title, *Blood Red the Sun*. Coppock agreed to take care of the publishing end of the project and once all expenses had been covered, he and Cameron were to share the profits equally. When the book appeared in the spring of 1950 it carried an introduction by Owen Wister, two additional chapters—"The Mutter of the Drums" and "Three Scouts"—and other alterations and rewriting. Cameron was tireless in its promotion wherever he travelled.

By this time, having fallen in love with his old haunts around Loon Lake and Meadow Lake, Saskatchewan, he moved there from British Columbia but never managed to recapture the mood he had known in his youth. He lived at Loon Lake in summer and Meadow Lake or North Battleford in winter—or at least he would have done so had his old friend "Chum" Craig had his way. Craig, a bachelor and running one of the Craig Company's chain stores in North Battleford, lived in a large house and offered to put Cameron up anytime he wished.[19]

Cameron's letters to his son Douglas were revealing at this stage of his life.[20] They spoke more of the difficulties of writing, of heart trouble, and of the long cold winters. His son expressed surprise at the mention of age by his father who had previously never given it a thought.

Living alone in a converted store in Meadow Lake, the old Indian trader was finally subdued by the bitter winter of 1950-51. His son received a telegram in Montreal in early March stating that Cameron was in hospital in bad condition. Douglas caught the earliest flight available and headed west into a region beset by blizzards and terrible road conditions. With the help of friends, and a battle through a hundred and ten miles of drifted roads to Meadow Lake, he arrived to find Cameron still alive but comatose. As Douglas spoke to him he gave an almost imperceptible nod and then died from the effects of double pneumonia. The date was March 4, 1951.

Cameron left little in worldly goods. His son, in settling the estate, found the living quarters "absolutely bare and cheerless . . . an awful ordeal to have to go back and sort and pack his personal effects in such surroundings." Cameron left a battered typewriter, a trunk full of books, scrapbooks, letters and manuscripts, no debts, and a balance of $62 in a bank account. The veteran's pension had been increased to $50, and Douglas, who had sent him money from time to time over his mild protests, estimated that his father's income from writing toward the end brought in another $200 per year.[21] Like many before him and since, Cameron had learned that freelance writing in the United States was one thing, in Canada entirely different.

William Bleasdell Cameron lies buried at Meadow Lake, Saskatchewan, amongst those who knew his worth and surrounded by the pleasant countryside he loved so much. Significantly, it is not far from the scene in which he played the most important part in his life.

As a writer, Cameron's most productive period came between his arrival in the North-West Territories in 1881 and 1899, by which time he had written the manuscript for *The War Trail of Big Bear*, even though it remained unpublished for many years. Behind him he left hundreds of articles in the quality journals of the United States, Great Britain, and Canada.

After 1900 when Cameron was drawn back to the North-West by the land boom, he wrote very little for a considerable period as he plunged into one business venture after another, finally becoming a travelling salesman. From this position he was rescued by the publication of *The War Trail of Big Bear* in 1926. From that point on, Cameron was a recognized and a committed author, suffering the ups and downs with other writers in Canada and, with them, being forced from time to time to take up other occupations to survive.

Cameron tried writing fiction but despite encouragement — mainly from his friend Owen Wister — his heart wasn't in it.[22] The simple reason was that he was a man of fact. That made him a journalist, a reporter. Hence he was captivated by what he saw from the time he first arrived in the Territories. He saturated himself with the land and its people, quickly absorbing the essence of the new countryside that set it apart from others.

As a result, his writings dealt with the fur trade, Indians, their leaders, tribal customs, and the North-West Mounted Police. He lived among the natives and with them and his short descriptive passages which humanized them are by far his best work. In the case of Indians, he categorized them and equated them with other leaders in the vast panorama of human history. Some he placed on a high plane, level with the heroes of the Old World.

Napoleon is reputed to have asked the rhetorical question: "What is history but a fable agreed upon?" This may be true of some, but not of Cameron's accounts. Reviewers, academics, and journalists have praised Cameron's power of honest observation and his ability to use it in his sturdy and entertaining prose. Professor A. S. Morton, historian and head of the history department of the University of Saskatchewan, introduced Cameron at a meeting of the Saskatchewan Historical Society in 1928, saying, "I realized when I had dinner with him, the value of getting him [to speak], for his knowledge of the place was from within, not casual."[23] Father Laurant Legoff, O.M.I., summarized the essence of all the other observers, providing a testament to Cameron's integrity and honest reporting. A missionary who indirectly escaped death at Frog Lake himself, he later wrote an account in French entitled "During the Rebellion." The translater states, "Father Legoff knew Mr. Cameron and was of the firm opinion that such a man *could* only speak the truth."[24]

The dramatic impact of Cameron's Frog Lake account has tended to draw attention away from his shorter pieces. In fact they all fit together, his books and articles, to constitute a body of work that makes a respectable factual contribution to the western story.

Where does one turn to read what it was like to sit around a campfire smoking a peace pipe? When an Indian trader set out to an Indian encampment, what goods did he take to tempt them to give up their furs or treaty money? These and countless other questions are answered in the bright and memorable accounts by Cameron.

His works have an advantage few contemporary observers possessed: his impressions were not filtered through the mind of any interpreter. He was a master of Cree and spoke to the Indians as man to man in their own language, innocent of racial prejudice. There is none of the white superiority over the "child-like" native in Cameron's works. He had only one view—the direct one. Written at a time when Americans, Britons, and eastern Canadians were so curious about this new, this unknown country that they would buy everything he wrote, these honest and candid memoirs are still eminently readable. Today they are doubly important because the culture they describe is no more, the personalities have vanished. Fortunately, Cameron was there at the time as a first hand observer and his works are his legacy.

For these and other reasons, we are fortunate to be able to reach back to the nineteenth century and mingle with the traders and Indians as if it were only yesterday. This is made possible, as well as instructive and entertaining, by the preservation of the eyewitness accounts of William Bleasdell Cameron, *N-Chawamis.*

I

ELEMENTS
OF THE ADVENTURE

When Bleasdell Cameron first arrived in Winnipeg, the North-West Territories contained little more than 50,000 people—natives, mixed bloods, and whites. It was virtually an empty land. There were a few sparsely populated centres west of Winnipeg which, Cameron found upon arrival, were in the midst of a land boom. Existing communities owed their origins to the Hudson's Bay Co., missionary stations, Mounted Police posts, or to varying combinations of the three.

Battleford, the Territorial capital, was one such centre, as was Fort Edmonton. Others included Forts Ellice, Qu'Appelle, Carlton, Pitt, and Fort Macleod. Perhaps the most populous centre, with about three thousand people, was Prince Albert. It started as a Presbyterian mission near an HBC post, and soon was joined by the Anglican church and a NWMP detachment. Fifty miles south was Batoche, on the South Saskatchewan River, a Metis population centre and river crossing on the important Carlton Trail linking that fort with distant Winnipeg.

At one time the western prairies were black with millions of grazing buffalo, providing sustenance for natives and Metis hunters. Not any more. By 1881, with the opening of the American West by railways, the herds had been wiped out by commercial hunters, often for their hides alone. By 1881, the sight of a single buffalo was a rarity in the Territories. The land was on the verge of massive change.

The Trail of '81

On a bright warm afternoon in late July, 1881, Verey and I turned west from Main Street, Winnipeg, and, with the ungreased axle of our highwheeled Red River cart screeching like a lost soul in purgatory, plodded beside Verey's red-and-white ox out along the Portage road, wilderness bent.

The Portage road, which was the highway to Portage la Prairie, is now Portage Avenue, and you may reach one side from the other, either of it or of Main Street, without risking your footwear. But those were the days when the future Manitoban metropolis was a raw border town, famed chiefly for the glutinous quality of its mud, and the crossing of one of its thoroughfares after a rain without losing at least your rubbers was an achievement, and possibly front page news for the *Free Press*.

The Marquis of Lorne, governor-general of Canada and Queen Victoria's son-in-law, had passed through Winnipeg, westbound like Verey and me, a week ahead of us, and everybody knew of it; but our arrival occasioned no perceptible ripple of excitement. A day or two later I met Sandy Macdonald and Ad McPherson. Sandy, who, although he has passed on, still lives in the name above the portals of numerous wholesale grocery establishments in the West, was then a small jobber in foodstuffs on Main Street; McPherson was loading goods for Battleford and Fort Edmonton, at both of which points the Winnipeg man had an interest in trading posts. I became then and there the hireling of the future sugar-and-spice millionaire, assigned to the former post, and Macdonald arranged with the guileful McPherson that Verey and I should journey westward under his experienced wing. This was supposed to ensure us freedom from alarms, but as a matter of

Reprinted from The Beaver, *Winnipeg, Man., March 1943.*

fact the chief source of such alarms as assailed us during the two or three weeks I travelled with him was Ad himself. "Charlie" Ross, in reality James Ross, was one of a half a dozen men who handled McPherson's train of a hundred loaded carts, and it is of interest to note that Hon. Frank Oliver and his bride of a week left Winnipeg for Edmonton with an outfit hauled by cattle just a few days before us.

McPherson was in camp on Colony Creek, out along the Portage road, and we pitched our tent near his on what was then open prairie but is now a thickly populated section of the city. We had two weeks to wait. Ad was busy. A grizzled halfbreed, expert at the job, was adding required carts to his string as fast as he could make them, while McPherson himself was occupied in familiarizing a couple of dozen steers fresh off the range with the rule of the road.

A steer was roped, brought up and secured—objections summarily overruled—between the shafts of a cart packed to the brim with sheet tin. Unheeded, the steer, under the delusion that he was once more free, and smarting from the indignities heaped upon him, with an outraged bawl started off. The cart, lunging after, brought him to a startled halt. With a bewildered look over his shoulder, he lurched suddenly to the left. His tow followed. Panic then seized him. To be spanked soundly by a ton of tin is no joke, even for a deep-chested upstanding steer, and away he streaked with the cart, shedding bundled tin at every spring, bounding and rattling behind him, and with McPherson, mounted, whip in hand and yelling like an Apache, hot on his heels.

But such a frenzied pace could not last, and at a distance of a few hundred yards, spent and blown, the pupil came to a staggering stop. After that it was no great task for Ad to herd him back to camp. Two or three such lessons were enough to temper the spirits of the wildest steer. Thereafter he was readily broken to the labour of the trail.

McPherson at last had all the carts he needed, with ponies and oxen educated to pull them; another day or two for final preparations and we should be headed into the sunset, with Battleford, six hundred miles away, our first objective, and Fort Edmonton, three hundred miles farther on, at the end of the trail.

The day had been suffocatingly hot—one of those sticky, oppressive days when only to stir is a burden—and we all sprawled in the shade of the carts, listless and uncomfortable. The air was pulseless. Suppertime came. A wind blew up out of the east, a wind soft, gratefully refreshing. Abruptly the sky in the west went black. The sun was blotted out. Clouds sullen, leaden, gathered quickly, mounting and spreading; the wind veered, blowing suddenly from the clouds, and as suddenly it was cold. There was the rumble of approaching thunder, and a few raindrops, big as marbles, struck like bullets on the hard, parched earth.

McPherson had bounced out of his tent. "Draw the cart-covers taut! Lash the buckboard to the carts—tie everything down tight! She's goin' to blow!" he shouted, dashing about the camp, yanking on a rope-end here, swinging an axe on a tent peg there, goading his men to a furious activity.

And blow she did! Everything above the grass bowed and staggered. Canvas thrashed, carts creaked, ropes writhed and whined in the roaring wind. The ground shook under the resounding blows of the thunder and in the incessant glare of the lightning the silent camp stood out as clear as day. Rain fell in tons out of the sodden sky and the flat plain beneath swam in the flood inches deep. The stock stood, backs to the storm, with heads lowered, patiently awaiting its passing.

For four hours the bombardment kept up, and through it all Verey lay quietly in our tent with his head pillowed on a case of surgical instruments. Verey was English and a sailorman. He had a brother at Fort Edmonton—Dr. Verey, perhaps the future capital's first medical man. The sailor was taking a holiday from the sea to pay his brother a visit and was bringing along the instruments as a gift.

While the storm raged, Verey occupied the tent alone with the instruments. I was willing he should. It was wet outside but, I considered, safer. And I had hardly recovered from the shock I'd got when knocked down a few months before by lightning in the East.

"Why don't you get out? With all that steel beside you in the tent, you're liable to get hurt." I said to him.

Verey grunted. "If you're going to be killed you'll be killed, steel or no steel, and that's all there is to it. You can't do anything by moving around." A moment later he was asleep.

That storm on Colony Creek was, I believe, the most terrific I have ever witnessed. We learned next day that two men, holding up their tent at Brandon when it was at its peak, had been struck by lightning and killed.

At Portage la Prairie I picked up a team of horses belonging to Mr. Macdonald, and from that point on I drove the buckboard, leaving to Verey the sole and undisputed management of his ox. We did, however, continue in joint occupancy of the tent when in camp.

Ad McPherson usually rode with me at the head of the long crawling procession of the cart train, yarning of his own colourful earlier youth on both sides of the international border, while I listened, fascinated. He told stories of construction days on the Union Pacific Railway which he helped to build, when the men worked with rifles beside them to stand off surprise attacks from hostile Indians; of his career as a foot-racer in Montana when the ordinary stake, which as a rule he won, was a fat poke of gold dust; of his first trip to the North Saskatchewan in '69 with Black Jack and Dancing Bill. On that occasion Bull's Head, the towering chief of the Sarcees, with a dozen of his braves, halted them at a point which would now approximate Wetaskiwin, demanding payment before they would be allowed to cross "his land;" and, upon being liberally paid in tobacco, threateningly demanded more, emphasizing his terms by commencing to pull his gun out of its "coat." Whereupon Ad, then a youth of eighteen, to the consternation of his companions who were hurrying to comply with the fresh requisitions, whipped out a pistol and ordered the one-eyed potentate to leave the "coat" on. Bull's Head, grinning, did so and the party moved on to "Edmington"—always "Edmington" to Ad—without the payment of further tribute. Bull's Head professed to regard the matter as a joke. Subsequent events proved, however, that he had not forgotten—or forgiven—the boy who pulled a gun on him. But that is another story.

There never will be another Ad McPherson. The wild adventurous years that fashioned characters like him are gone forever. He was typically representative of that vanished time. A Virginian by birth and orphaned at an early age, while still a youngster he had slipped out of the custody of the uncle who had adopted him and struck for the West. He was about thirty when I first met him, of medium height, compact build, with a red face, fiery red hair, a bristling red moustache, snapping humorous blue eyes and a short nose to which nature had imparted a comically pugnacious tilt. He had little education and his utterances at times were simply lurid and appalling. Yet there was about him always a certain courtliness and customarily a subtle distinction of speech and manner that betokened a descent of which no one would have need to be ashamed.

At Fort Ellice, by trail two hundred miles and by water probably double that distance from Winnipeg, I parted from McPherson and my seafaring mate, Verey, in anticipation of a stay of some weeks. In that day the Assiniboine River was navigated from its mouth at Winnipeg as far up as Fort Ellice by flat-bottomed stern-wheelers. I had been instructed by Mr. Macdonald to await at Fort Ellice the arrival of a number of halfbreed freighters, who were to come down from the Saskatchewan River settlements to meet the boats bringing goods up to Ellice for my employer's Battleford post.

Fort Ellice, an old and important establishment of the Hudson's Bay Company, at that time was headquarters of the Swan River District and of Chief Factor Archibald McDonald, the district officer in charge. Mrs. McDonald was a sister of the Hon. Colin Inkster, for fifty years sheriff at Winnipeg.

Fort Ellice was perched on the level prairie high above and overlooking the broad valley of the Assiniboine, from wall to wall of which the strongly flowing river wound a sinuous course. Quite early one morning we heard the distant blast of a steamboat and the whole population flocked to the bank before the fort to see above the tree tops down the valley a thin plume of smoke. But the boat herself did not show up at her mooring berth soon by any means. From nine o'clock until after noon we watched that feathery streamer weaving back and forth across the valley. In a direct line the vessel, when we first sighted her, could not have been more than five miles away, but she must have steamed fifteen to reach the landing. A second boat followed.

The cargoes were duly delivered on the mud bank, and thence stored in the large warehouse of the Hudson's Bay Company in the valley, pending the appearance of the freighters. I secured lodgings at the home of Henry Bastien, the Company's warehouseman, and having nothing to do until the carts arrived, put in the time tramping the hills and valleys of the Assiniboine and its affluent, the Qu'Appelle, with my gun. I seldom returned to my quarters without a good bag of ducks or prairie chickens, or both. At Fort Ellice, too, I saw for the last time those beautiful game birds that as a small boy I had hunted in the East, where they were then to be found in flocks of thousands, but which, so far as is known, have for thirty years or so been extinct—passenger pigeons. To discover a pair of them, one morning shortly after my arrival, in the scrub oaks not far below the fort, certainly gave me a surprise.

There were other things of interest at Fort Ellice. Here, for example, I had my first view of the noble red man of the plains before contact with the effette pale-face had robbed him of his picturesqueness. A band of Sioux, with many horses, were in camp along a coulee not far from the fort. Often, gorgeous in paint, feathers and many-hued blankets, they strutted about, silent spectators of that strange creature, the white man, and his amazing activities. When they watered their horses they usually rode into the valley naked except for their breechclouts, with buffalo robes thrown over their shoulders.

At length Solomon Venne, with his big brigade of carts and a number of other halfbreeds, turned up at Ellice, and after loading them I was ready to take the trail for Battleford. I was now joined by two other Macdonalds, Ronald and Robert, who also had a team and buckboard. There had already been a quite heavy fall of snow before we left Fort Ellice on October 13, and the fine warm weather which had earlier made a joy of travelling was now lacking. Apart from the novelty of viewing for the first time a vast new land and day by day drawing farther and farther away from civilization and deeper into the wilderness, the second lap of my journey to Battleford did not promise much of entertainment.

Until we had made a hundred miles west we saw no settlement, but beside the blue lakes in the smiling Qu'Appelle valley a few halfbreed buffalo hunters were cultivating patches of the prodigal soil about their log shacks, and we overtook one or two Ontario families, with all their worldly goods loaded on oxen, westward bound in quest of homes in this rich virgin territory. We passed the Hudson's Bay Company and North-West Mounted Police posts at Fort Qu'Appelle thirty miles farther on, and after another fifty miles broke our journey to rest our tired horses and pass a pleasant day under the hospitable roof of W. Muirhead, manager of Heubach's trading post in the Touchwood Hills. The weather had continued wintry, with around zero temperatures, and snow covered the ground.

We made the South Saskatchewan at Clark's Crossing a few days later at ten o'clock at night, with a prairie fire reflected from a clouded sky upon the surrounding landscape showing the way and enabling us to travel long after ordinarily we should have been snug in our blankets. With milder temperatures the snow had vanished.

After ferrying over the river, our trails parted. The main line of the Canadian Pacific across the prairies had not yet been located so far west, but a trial survey had been run to The Elbow of the river, eighty miles south of Clark's, and it was believed the railway would span the big stream at that point. The Macdonalds were hurrying to The Elbow to "squat" on land in anticipation of its being required for townsite purposes and becoming valuable. Ultimately the line passed fifty miles south of The Elbow—and no one ever made a fortune out of Elbow city lots.

My course lay west thirty miles to another Elbow, that of the North Saskatchewan, and thence, following the river, sixty more miles to Battleford.

The day the Macdonalds left me I, too, had my troubles. Shortly before sundown, when crossing a slough, the ice suddenly parted under me and, like McGinty in the song, down I went to the bottom, with the result that, again like McGinty, I was "very wet." I need only add that eventually I got out, but not until after I had plunged my arms to the shoulders under the freezing surface to loosen the harness and free the horses, which by this time had acquired a "what's-the-use" complex and refused to make further effort to save themselves, leaving it up to me to drag them almost bodily to dry land. Following this I stumbled through the broken ice with all my effects to shore and then by mighty effort pulled the empty buckboard out myself.

It was now dark, a cold wind blew from the west across the flat open plain and, to put warmth and life into my stiffened and benumbed steeds, with my garments rattling like boards on my shrinking frame, I drove on along the old government telegraph line for an hour. Then, of a sudden, to my intense relief there flashed before my straining eyes the gleam of a camp fire. In no time I pulled up beside it. Two men, line repairers from Battleford, were warming themselves there. They bustled about, threw me a change of clothing, filled me to the Plimsoll mark with bacon and eggs and made me a comfortable shakedown for the night. I went on next morning, and after four more endless days on an exclusive diet of cold flapjacks (I've never been able to face a flapjack since without a shudder), arrived in Battleford, sixteen days from Fort Ellice, on October 29.

Thirty years later I stepped aboard a sleeper in the magnificent Canadian National station at Winnipeg and in a little over twenty-four hours, covering practically the same route, stepped off again in the new town of North Battleford. In 1881 the trip had required more than that many days.

The Romance of Pemmican

In the month of June, 1899, the Government of Canada invited tenders for the supply of a quantity of pemmican to be used by that substantial division of the North-West Mounted Police quartered in the mining district of the Yukon. The quantity required was ten tons, and bids were invited for the supply of the whole or any portion of it. It was to be put up in fifty-pound rawhide sacks and to be of three qualities: the first, for human consumption, made from good steers and cows, and the second and third from bulls and coarse cattle and fat, healthy horses, for the sustenance of the transport equipment of the Yukon division—the trains of big "Huskie" sled dogs, animals best fitted to the purposes of winter travel in the inhospitable corners of the North.

That the tenderers were few seems probable from the fact that the pemmican was manufactured, during the following months of July and August, by the Mounted Police themselves, or rather by halfbreeds and Indians under supervision of members of the Force. Some five tons were put up at Duck Lake, on the Saskatchewan River. Nearly a hundred head of cattle were purchased in the district and turned over to Joseph Parenteau, an old French-Cree halfbreed buffalo hunter, who had contracted at a cent a pound for the manufacture of the pemmican.

Parenteau engaged Cree Indians from the adjacent reserves to do the actual work, for which they received as payment the heads and offal of the slaughtered animals. A sergeant-major of the Mounted Police was on hand to superintend operations and see that no tainted or foreign ingredients went into the product.

Reprinted from The Canadian Magazine, *Toronto, Ont., March* *1902.*

Fifty years earlier pemmican was, to the shifting and scant population of the North-West, what flour is in the present day to English-speaking peoples in most civilized portions of the globe—the staple and most common food of the country. Then it was always made from the buffalo which covered the western plains. The great fur corporation known as the Hudson's Bay Company bought hundreds of bags of the dark, nutritious compound annually from the Indians, for use at its trading posts scattered over the vast wilderness stretching from Red River and Hudson Bay to the Rocky Mountains and from the two Saskatchewans to the Arctic Sea, a region then designated as Rupert's Land.

Pemmican (or, more properly, *pimeekon*) is a Cree word, meaning a mixture, or something made with fat. It was composed of buffalo meat dried in the sun and pounded fine, mixed with melted fat; and was sewn up in sacks made from the rawhide of the buffalo, with the hair outside. It did not look inviting, but was in fact wholesome, strong food, which would keep for years. Besides owing to its compactness, it was easily transported, an important consideration in the fur trade—particularly to the tripper and voyageur, whether by dog-sled, canoe or York boat.

Flour, in those times, was something the great Company's servant seldom saw; a small cake or two at Christmas was a rare treat. And tea was little less of a luxury. But, as pemmican was plenty, the absence of these things was scarcely a deprivation to him, and the rugged Orkneyman or swart halfbreed, seated by the bank of some mighty inland stream or crouched in the snow over his campfire of willows beside the frozen highway of the wilds, ate his chunk of the packed meat and drank his tin "pot" of cold water with great relish, perhaps, even than the fastidious clubman disposed of his dinner and wine at his fashionable Gotham or London club. What was good enough for Jack was good enough for his master, too, and no Hudson's Bay Company's officer or clerk would despise a piece of good pemmican.

But if the buffalo was important to the fur trader, the ungainly animal was life itself to the red man; for it furnished him with everything his heart could desire or with the means of procuring it. And as, owing to the migratory instincts of the herds, which took them first into the recognized territory of one tribe and next into that of an enemy, fresh meat was not always obtainable, pemmican was the form in which the Indian preserved and laid away his store of provisions against the day of scarcity.

Omitting the excitement of the hunt and substituting domestic herds for the wild ones of the plains, a description of pemmican-making by the Indians a quarter of a century ago will give an idea of what might have been witnessed at Duck Lake in the summer of 1899.

Intelligence that a band of buffalo was in the vicinity threw the Indian camp at once into a state of violent excitement. Men rushed from the lodges, buckling on quivers of arrows and belts of cartridges, women talked and gesticulated, boys raced wildly about shouting shrilly to one another, the horse herd was driven in, and in a few minutes the bucks, mounted on their "buffalo-runners" and under the direction of the chief of the hunt, moved in a silent body out of the camp.

On nearing the herd, advantage was taken of each slight rise or dip to cover the approach, which was always up wind, so that the wary brutes should not catch the scent. Stealthily they rode, one behind another, until concealment was no longer possible. Then, at a signal from the chief, they burst upon the open plain, and dashed, yelling, at the top speed of their trained horses at the startled herd.

Usually it was some distance away—perhaps half a mile—and it took a good horse to overhaul a buffalo. Once up with the straining animals, however, their pace slackened, and the rest was comparatively easy. Onward galloped the hunters between the long, undulating files of shaggy, brown backs, picking out the fat cows and the young bulls at their leisure. And, as a feathered shaft left the snapping bowstring and a stricken beast tottered and went down, the loud, triumphant cry of the hunter rang out, and he tossed a moccasin or a beaded firebag beside it to mark his kill, and then flew on.

The chase might last as long as the horses' wind. When it was over the women came with the ponies and the trailing travois upon the field of slaughter. The carcasses were soon stripped of their hairy coats, the meat packed on the travois, the bones broken and the marrow extracted, and, loaded with the red spoil, the whole party returned to camp. Here, in an incredibly short time, the meat was cut into wide, thin sheets, and hung upon pole frames in the sun and wind to dry.

After a day or two these sheets were removed and spread upon the clean prairie grass, where, if the weather continued fair, they soon became as hard as shingles. They were then placed upon a hide threshing floor with the sides elevated on short pegs to form a sort of basin and beaten with flails or between stones until the meat was reduced almost to a powder. The strange thing was that if properly handled the flesh seldom, if ever, became at all tainted, though in any other than the dry, pure atmosphere of the

North-West such a method of preparing it would doubtless be impossible.

Meanwhile, the marrow and other choice fat had been rendered, and bags, some two feet by one and a half, of raw buffalo hide doubled over at the bottom and sewn up the sides with the sinew of the animal, made for the reception of the pemmican. The melted fat was next poured over the shredded meat in the threshing basin and the whole mixed to the consistency of paste. That was the pemmican.

It was shovelled into the sacks, pounded down, and after the tops had been sewn up and the bags jumped upon to make them flat, the cooled pemmican packages were as solid and almost as hard as so many boulders. When you desired to eat pemmican you chopped a piece off with an axe, sack and all. The meat was already cooked in a measure by sun, wind and the hot fat, but if you preferred, after tearing off the adhering hide, you could fry it in a pan or boil it in a pot.

Only the leanest meat is used for pemmican. That which is streaked with fat and, therefore, will not get hard enough to pulverize well, is called dried meat. It is cut and cured in sheets like the other, but is afterward folded up and tied, half a dozen sheets together, into bales two feet square. Like pemmican the dried meat is nutritious, but it is not quite so palatable, especially if it has been made for a long time. Nor does it keep as well.

Such, twenty years ago (1880), was pemmican making on the plains. Shooting cattle was tame sport compared with the buffalo chase, but when in 1900 the Indians learned of the call for tenders, they spoke together of the bountiful dead past and came two hundred miles to feast and look on. For days the sheets of rich beef hung warping in the sun, and by night the tom-toms beat and quaint wild chants rose above a hundred camp fires.

Eighty-six animals, in all, were slaughtered, representing some 60,000 pounds of dressed fresh beef. From this was secured two tons, each of first and second class pemmican, and one ton of dried meat, a total of 10,000 pounds. As the latter figures represent the full food product (including the tongues, which are dried) and nutritive strength of the eighty-six animals, it will be at once seen what an economical form of provision, for transportation purposes, pemmican is. When it is further recollected that in any moderately temperate climate it will keep for years, the idea suggests itself that pemmican might be a useful addition to the commissariat of a military campaign such as the British are now conducting in South Africa [the Boer War].

As nearly as may be estimated without official data, the cost to the Canadian Government of the pemmican made at Duck Lake—each pound of which was the equivalent of six pounds of fresh beef—would be about forty cents per pound.

In the winter of 1881-2 I bought fifty pounds of pemmican from a halfbreed trader, for use on a 200-mile trip along the North Saskatchewan River. It had been made by the Blackfoot Indians and occasional buffalo hairs or stalks of dry grass were found in it. Yet I have made many such trips since, and on none of them have I eaten meat more wholesome, sustaining, or that I more thoroughly enjoyed than my 50-pound lump of pemmican. The halfbreeds make a preparation of it which they call "rubaboo." The pemmican is mixed with flour and water, seasoned and stewed in a frying pan. This I found the most appetizing form in which to eat it.

In the Athabasca and Mackenzie River districts of the Far North, the Indians make a pemmican of moose and caribou flesh, mixed with dried wild fruit. It is called "berry pemmican," and I have heard it compared with English plum pudding. But the true "pemmican days" have gone with many other of the most picturesque features of the old North-West life. Only the counterfeit remains.

Cart Transportation
in the Early West

The story of transportation in the early days of the Canadian North-West would make a fascinating book. To breathe into the subject the atmosphere of adventure and romance in which the rugged frontiersman threaded the mighty wilderness of plain and forest, mountain and waterway stretching from the St. Lawrence on the east to the Fraser and the Columbia on the west, such a volume would be a large one. In an article such as this it is possible only to touch here and there on particular phases of this pioneer business of transferring people, pelts and merchandise from one point to another over the wide empty spaces that separated the isolated trading posts and the stout little settlements then dotting that vast and silent land.

As a beginning, take the Red River cart, perhaps the most useful and ingenious piece of mechanism ever devised by a primitive people for purposes of transportation on land.

The genesis of the Red River cart is obscure. Just when, where or by whom it was invented seems in doubt. Possibly a resourceful halfbreed with a mechanical bent drew his inspiration from a two-wheeled contraption imported by some Hudson's Bay Company chief officer at great expense via the Straits of Hudson to dazzle the natives. Or it may have come from a *cabriolet magnifique* brought in pieces and in a "double-north" canoe up the Ottawa and over the Great Lakes all the way from old Quebec.

But whatever its origin, throughout the nineteenth century at least it was in common use and with the saddle horse as auxiliary, the chief means of transportation over the enormous territory between the Red River and the Rocky Mountains. At every

Reprinted from The Western Producer, *Saskatoon, Sask., December 1, 1949.*

Hudson's Bay Company post of importance in the valleys of the Red, the Assiniboine, the Qu'Appelle, and both the North and the South Saskatchewan rivers, there was certain to be a number of these crude-looking but extremely strong and serviceable carts, and when provisions ran short a small party under an employee of the post was sent from Carlton House, Fort Pitt, Victoria or Fort Edmonton out to the plains with goods in carts to be traded to Cree or Blackfoot hunters for pemmican, robes and meat.

Before the passing of the buffalo, the halfbreed hunters also used the carts for transport on their annual hunting expeditions to the plains, where the shaggy wild cattle roamed in herds of unnumbered thousands. And those Indian hunters with a sense of thrift, too, customarily counted among their possessions a cart or so in which to stow their effects when moving camp.

But it was in the transportation of merchandise to the remote posts of "the Great Company," not only from Fort Garry but even upon occasion from points as distant as St. Paul, Minnesota, that the Red River cart reached its highest plane of usefulness. Freighting was largely in the hands of the French halfbreeds, for whom the free, roving life of the open trail had an irresistible lure, and the native owner of fifty or a hundred carts, with the animals to pull them, was accounted a man of wealth and social eminence. And if his manner showed that in his view this estimate indicated intelligence of a high order among his compatriots, who will blame him? Most of us, if we will admit it, are a little vain.

Red River carts were for the most part made by halfbreeds adept at the work at White Horse Plain and other points on the Red and Assiniboine rivers adjacent to Winnipeg. They were built entirely of wood, the only metal about them being the bushings inside hubs and possibly an odd nail in the flooring. Wheels as well as axles were of oak. They had a diameter of some five feet and a pronounced concave "dish." The rim was formed of sections about two and a half feet long by four inches wide, shaped like bows or arcs. Holes bored in the ends, into which were driven stout oak pins, held the sections firmly together. Six or eight sections were required to complete the circle of the rim and two spokes went to a section.

The wheel had no tire and the half-inch gaps between the sections allowed for expansion or contraction of the rim as the season proved wet or dry. If a split occurred and a part of a section dropped off, the damage was readily repaired. The freighter was never without a roll of *babiche*—a raw oxhide scraped bare of hair—and from this a strip a couple of inches wide and as many feet long was cut. *Babiche* was thick and stiff as board. The strip was soaked until pliable, the broken piece was replaced and the *babiche* wound tightly round the break and a nail driven into the end to keep everything in position. As the wrapper dried it shrank to the wood and when it had regained its original stiffness the break was as rigidly fixed as if held in a vise.

The shafts extended the full length of the cart, which was ten or twelve feet. Like the wheels and the axle they were of oak, thick and heavy. Above the wheels sat the box or body, which carried the load. This was about five feet square, floored and sided with boards and bound firmly round the top by a wooden railing.

The harness was a simple affair: a collar and hames to which were attached short heavy leather "tugs" with half-inch iron "thole pins" at their ends. These pins fitted into holes running vertically through the shafts, where they were held by stout leather tie strings. On the back of the ox or pony rested a "clubber" or small stuffed saddle, over the top of which ran a heavy leather strap, ending in a loop on either side which supported the shafts. A second strap from the clubber along the back supported the breeching, through the iron rings at the ends of which the thole pins passed when the animal was harnessed, enabling him to hold back his load when descending a hill. No bridle or headgear was used on an ox, although there might be a rope around the base of his horns by which to fasten him to the cart ahead when on the move. Ponies were sometimes fitted with bridles, but in a cart train they customarily followed loose, one behind another. The load for a pony was usually eight to nine hundred pounds and for an ox two to three hundred more.

While the Red River cart was primarily a freight vehicle, there were times when it carried a passenger or two or an Indian and his family, in which case canvas-covered bows sometimes sheltered the occupants. The bridle of the pony hauling it was equipped with reins. Waterproof covers tied over the loads in a freight brigade protected them from the weather.

The start from Winnipeg was made as a rule in late July or early August. There were always loose animals, usually ponies, with a brigade of any size, to replace those playing out, acquiring sore backs or shoulders, going lame or meeting with accidents. Another purpose for which these loose animals might be used was to aid those in the carts over soft spots in the trail and up steep hills and the banks of streams. The method in practice was as follows:

A halfbreed, mounted, placed himself in front of the horse in a loaded cart. A rope, half-hitched to a thole pin of the cart at one end and to a loop made in the tail of the pony under him at the other, was the only doubling-up connection. At the word "Go!" the ponies started off together with a rush and up the hill or through the sludge sailed the cart, with the pony ahead, his rider drumming a tattoo on his ribs with his moccasined heels, buckling into the drag as whole-heartedly as his partner in the rear. This was repeated until the difficulty, whatever it might have been, was behind the brigade and there was smooth trail ahead once again.

The first time I witnessed this proceeding — one horse extending his tail as a helping hand to brothers in distress — it struck me as fiendishly cruel. Later I concluded I must be mistaken. The animal seemingly — to me — so inhumanly treated took to the job like a physical culture enthusiast to his daily dozen, nor could I discover that it did him any injury.

If bread is the staff of life, bacon in those days ran it a close second as provender, and in every sizeable freight shipment there was certain to be a liberal proportion of "sowbelly" — to give it the then popular title. It came in great slabs or sides and in coarse jute sacks, not in the small sections enveloped in many wrappings familiar to us of the present. Nor was it the delectable product that, superbly crisped, tempts us at the breakfast table. Sowbelly was cured in brine and was so salty that it invariably called for parboiling before it could be eaten.

But aside from its value as food, sowbelly could be put to purposes which would spell simple annihilation for its less robust successor. When a bad spot in the trail halted the caravan, the bacon loads — storm troops of the freight brigade — were rushed to the front, the heavy sacks lifted out and laid side by side across the treacherous ground and, thus corduroyed, the carts passed safely over instead of sinking to their axles in it. The extemporized bridge was picked up, stowed away and the brigade moved on. I never heard that the quality of the bacon was improved by these rather frequent immersions. On the other hand, however, bacon was bacon in those days and I never heard that the soakings disqualified it as merchandise for the trader to whom it was consigned or as food for his customers who bought it.

To a train of eighty to a hundred carts there were usually about half a dozen men, besides a cook and a night herder. The duties of the latter were to guard the stock from dusk to dawn to prevent its straying, being lost or run off by marauding Indians, halfbreeds or whites, and to bring it into camp at daybreak. The night herder, lulled by the strident music of some ungreased axle, got his rest during the day in a cart while the brigade travelled. Each man handled eight or ten carts when on the trail, walking between or alongside them, and his business was to catch and harness his allotted animals in the morning, unhitch when halts were called and keep them stepping when on the tramp. Fifteen miles was considered a good average day for a brigade, although some fast-walking ox-outfits (not too large) on shorter hauls, such as that between Fort Qu'Appelle and Battleford, on occasion averaged as much as twenty miles a day. The distance averaged by a large brigade, however, was more often half that, or ten miles a day.

The daily routine of a large brigade when on the trail followed somewhat this pattern:

The camp was awakened at dawn by the bawling of the cook, who often pounded a frying pan, and the men rolled out, packed and loaded their blankets, washed and ate breakfast. Meanwhile the animals had been driven by the night herder into a rope corral stretched around the carts. Those to be used were caught and tied and the others turned loose again. The harness was then put on the working animals, they were hitched to their loads and the brigade began to move. The carts in night camp were usually arranged in a circle — a Sioux or Blackfoot war party might suddenly appear from nowhere and it paid to take precautions. They started one after another out of the circle and passed in single file into the trail, the men shouting and cracking their whips to quicken their pace. Three or four hours were customarily as long as the brigade travelled to the first halt, about eleven o'clock. While the stock grazed, dinner — consisting of a stew of wild duck or prairie chicken perhaps, with a potato or two and an onion, bannock and possibly pie made from some wild fruit — was cooked and eaten and after a rest of a couple of hours the cart animals were again harnessed and the brigade was once more on the move.

About four o'clock the freighter, owner of the outfit, generally rode ahead to locate a spot where dry wood, water and grass provided the three essentials for a good night camp and if one was reached about that hour the brigade turned out of the trail and travel stopped for the day. But if he knew of another good camping ground not too far ahead, the outfit might go on for another hour, though seldom later than five o'clock. There was always a multitude of things waiting to be done after camp was made, most of them requiring daylight: broken harness and carts to be mended, galls on horses' backs and shoulders and about the base of the oxens' horns needing attention, shoes and clothing to be overhauled and, by the ultra fastidious, possibly shaving or even haircutting.

The night herder drove the stock off from the camp to graze, and supper disposed of, the men sat yarning and smoking about the campfire or gambling for tobacco. Perhaps a French halfbreed had brought his fiddle along and flung melody on the night breeze with "Drops of Brandy," the "Red River Jig," the "Duck Dance," or the "Reel de Huit." But weariness soon claimed them and by nine o'clock silence reigned, broken only by the sound of a horse clearing his nostrils, the bellow of a bullfrog, the shrill yapping of a single coyote that seemed a pack, the hum of mosquitoes, and snores from the sleeping men.

Day followed day as the brigade crawled on. Summer merged into fall. The nights grew longer. There was a hint of frost in the air and in the morning sun the stiffened grass-blades sparkled like spearpoints. With the coming of October ice began to form along the creek banks and in the water pail outside the cook tent. The animals in the carts, mere shadows of their earlier selves, dragged their wasted frames listlessly along. Came the first snow fall. And then, at last — Fort Edmonton!

Yes, it was a long, long road from Winnipeg to Edmonton in the 1870s and 1880s. Now the distance may be covered through the air in a matter of hours and minutes; then two months, with loads, was considered fast time. The North-West, with the rest of the world, has speeded up.

There were many other methods of pioneer transportation in the West — bull teams, four-horse teams, string teams, buckboards, saddles, pack trains, the stage coach, dogs, carrioles, flatsleds, travois, canoes, and finally York boats and steamboats — but there is no room for more than a mere catalogue of them here. Yet notwithstanding hardships — the exposure, the heat, the cold, the thousand and one inconveniences of the old trails, there must have been some compensations. It would be hard to say just what they were — perhaps a certain element of danger had something to do with it. All we know is that, by and large, we enjoyed it and would not have foregone those thrill-packed, adventurous days and nights along the old open trails, with the wild, free sweep of the plains all about us, for all the money in the world!

A Race for Life

The days when, from the Red River to the foothills of the Rocky Mountains, the Canadian West was a land of savage splendour—a vast verdant sea sweeping league on league to dim horizons—with the onward march of the years are receding farther and farther into the past, and those who breathed their glamour and romance are few, and rapidly becoming fewer. Soon even these will have entered the silence, and only on the printed page will the West that was still live.

But through the lips of one here and there of that swiftly vanishing handful it is yet possible upon occasion to catch glimpses of those stirring, departed days. Such a one is Mrs. McKay, who at the age of ninety-odd makes her home near Prince Albert. Mrs. McKay is the widow of that stout-hearted frontiersman, William McKay, one of the famous Hudson's Bay Company family of that name, a veteran Indian trader who closed his eyes in August of 1930 upon a region he had seen change from a mighty wilderness, over which warring Indian tribes and buffalo in unnumbered thousands roamed at will, into a land sown thickly with towns and carved throughout its broad extent into the pleasant farmsteads of peaceful and industrious settlers.

In these modern days, when little remains of the pioneer past, should one find himself suddenly possessed with a burning desire to beard the buffalo on his native heath, it would be necessary for him to journey to one of the government parks at Elk Island or Banff in Alberta. Even then he would have no assurance of excitement; he might find the great shaggy beasts—once the wild and, in some circumstances, dangerous monarchs of the plains —scarcely less tame or more formidable than the animals in a farmer's barnyard. But it was not always so, as Mrs. McKay is able

Reprinted from The Beaver, Winnipeg, Man., *March 1946*

out of her own experience to testify. Some years ago she gave me a vivid account of an adventure of those wild days in which she perforce took an active if unrelished part. She said:

I was a young girl then, my friend, living at Carlton House, the old Hudson's Bay district headquarters post on the North Saskatchewan, where my father, John Rowland, was in the service of the Great Company. Except the traders and a few missionaries, there were as yet no whites in the country. Even Prince Albert, one of the earliest settlements, had still to be born. Outside the stockades of the forts the red men, who were often insolent and unruly, still dominated the land.

It might be supposed that life at the fur posts, especially for the women, was dreary and monotonous, but we did not find it so. On the contrary, the time as a rule passed quickly and happily. Our household duties—including the making of our own clothes—kept us occupied, and for amusement we had dances, snowshoeing, skating and hunting (the latter usually in the winter and for rabbits), riding, berrying and horse- and dog-team racing. Visitors were frequent, too; there was always much travel between the posts. Major Butler, who wrote *The Great Lone Land*—later Sir William F. Butler—stayed with us more than once. And then there were the visits of the Indians, feathered and bedaubed with their brilliant paints, with furs and buffalo robes to trade. No, life at the posts was not dull. It was pleasant, often exciting. For one thing, we were not troubled, as in these difficult days, over money matters.

I had one ambition that, until I was almost full grown, I was unable to gratify. I had for long wished to go out to the plains to see a buffalo hunt and to watch the Indian women cutting up the meat and making pemmican, but I had failed to obtain my father's consent.

Attakakoop, "Star Blanket," one of the local chiefs, was a man of much authority, good character and responsibility, held in high esteem by my parent. At length I hit upon the idea of enlisting the aid of the chief. He was leaving with a party of his followers and a train of carts for the country south of Carlton to secure a supply of meat. I persuaded him to use his influence with my father to let me go along. On Star Blanket's promising that I should be brought safely back, I at last obtained the coveted permission. I was delighted.

But Attakakoop did not know the risk he ran in undertaking to return me in good repair to Carlton. I was certain of being returned, of course, but as it turned out I might easily have arrived without knowing anything about it.

We were headed for the Point of Woods, a lofty, grass-grown plateau studded with poplar clumps and sparkling blue lakes, which jutted out into the plain about half way between the present town of Battleford and the Eagle Creek. It was an ideal campground.

We journeyed along, living on the fat of the land (the country was full of game—blacktail deer, antelope, Canada geese, wavies, sandhill cranes and prairie chickens) until we reached a point opposite where the city of Saskatoon now stands, though west of the South Saskatchewan river and some distance from that stream. The country here was very dry, but one of the Indians told us of a spring he had once located in a coulee perhaps half a mile away, and I set off with Attakakoop's sister to fetch some water. She was an elderly woman and we both stayed in the chief's tent with his family. We carried two-gallon kegs on our shoulders, where they were held by straps passing round our foreheads.

The coulee, when we at last came to it, was wide and deep. We found the spring at the bottom, filled our kegs and began the stiff climb back. At the top we paused to recover our breath and rest.

The view—the vast shimmering plain drowsing in the sunlight; in the far distance a dark mass—a great herd of buffalo grazing—held me and I stood for some moments bewitched. A sharp exclamation from the old woman awoke me.

"Look out, my sister! He is wounded, that one." A moment's pause, then: "Run—*run!*"

I looked round quickly. I was wearing a red shawl. An immense buffalo bull a few hundred yards away was staring belligerently at me, now and then tossing his great shaggy head and pawing the ground. As I stared back at him, paralysed with fright, he suddenly lowered his head and charged.

"Run, O run, my sister!" shrieked the old woman. "I'm too old, I can't; but you may get away. If he is overtaking you, give him your shawl—throw it down!"

I had dropped my keg. I recovered my wits. I acted on the old woman's advice and ran—for my life! I ran till I thought my heart would burst. But it was of no use. The bull gained. He had plunged right over the old woman without ever seeing her. I flung off my shawl. The animal stopped, ripped it to pieces with his horns, trampled it under foot. Then he again rushed after me.

I had had a brief breathing space and I tore on, but he was soon again overtaking me. Hope died in me. Once more I was ready to drop. I fell. I closed my eyes. My lips moved in anguished prayer as I awaited the doom that was thundering down upon me. How could I ever forget those short swift seconds of suspense!

Then—a shout!—and, instantly following—a shot! What, *what* could it mean? I took courage, then, and raised my eyes—to see the great beast crash to the ground a few feet behind me!

I shook in every limb. A mounted man stood over me, a halfbreed hunter, Diomme Laboucan. He had from a distance seen the bull and my frantic race and, beating a tattoo on the ribs of his trained buffalo runner, had arrived just in the nick of time to save my life. His second shot had brought to an abrupt stop the bull's headlong pursuit.

At length I was able to move and, after thanking my rescuer haltingly out of a full heart, I rejoined the old woman. Then we picked up our kegs and made our way back to camp.

On arriving home some weeks later, with carts groaning under heaped-up loads of buffalo meat and pemmican, Attakakoop and his followers decided that, in gratitude to Manito for saving from a violent death the daughter of the white *Okemow*, nothing less than a grand celebration would serve properly to mark such a thrilling event. This duly came off. Over the centre pole of the big open lodge erected for the occasion floated fragments of the shawl, the flashing challenge of which had so maddened the wounded bull. Following the feasting and the shuffling of the warriors in the grass dance, the weird wild quaver in the voices of the drummers marking the time in the measured boom of the big drum, Attakakoop made a speech in which in glowing terms he lauded what he was pleased to call my "bravery." In turn I was asked to recount to the assembled tribesmen the details of my race and escape from the enraged bull, which I did in the best Cree at my command. At the same time I was thinking that it was Laboucan's resourcefulness and action in flying to my rescue that they should have been celebrating rather than my frenzied efforts to travel faster than the bull. It was long past midnight when the celebration ended.

Incidentally, my father did not think much of it all. I was told very pointedly that any more such excursions and adventures were definitely "out." He left me to infer what dire consequences would follow any infraction of this edict.

II

THE FUR TRADE

Through the author's observations and experiences, he was able to provide a birdseye view of the fur trade as it was, and to offer a fascinating glimpse into the life of a trapper in Canada's outposts—his work, his habits, and his survival.

Just a few years before Cameron's arrival, the Hudson's Bay Co. had transferred the land to the Canadian government; the pragmatic system of HBC law under which they had operated reasonably well for two hundred years was changed to another unfamiliar code. Whether a good or bad thing, it was unsettling. Cameron was in a position to gather stories of those earlier days, as well as to play his own role as an Indian trader during the changing times.

How Promotion Came to Fred Stanson

A Fictional Tale of the Hudson's Bay Territory

"Can you go, Francois?"

The trader, muffled in a fur coat, lay near the fire, between buffalo robes spread under the sloping roof of spruce boughs. He looked anxiously at the halfbreed whom he addressed. The man stood holding his hands outstretched over the blaze, and he did not shift his eyes from the coals as he replied doggedly after a moment's silence:

"The storm is wild. It is very cold and the way is long. There is no trail. It is not safe."

"But you, Gladieu?—Ah, you also are afraid."

He sunk his face in the robes with a despairing groan. He had one of his violent seizures of asthma. They occurred often during the heat, but rarely in winter, so that he had not thought to bring remedies on this trip to the hunting Indians. At the fort was a specific which gave him instant relief in such attacks; but the fort was forty miles away and a broad plain stretched between. They had had nothing to eat for the two days during which they had lain stormbound in this wood bluff on their way back.

"I will go." He was a well-knit, fairhaired young fellow that volunteered, and resolution spoke from his blue eyes.

"*You?*" The trader turned upon him a look of mingled incredulity and admiration. This stripling—for so he regarded him—to attempt what men, natives inured to hardship and knowing the plains like a map, ready for almost any risk, would not? It would be criminal of him to consider it.

"No, no; I thank you, Stanson, but I cannot consent. It would be a useless sacrifice; you could not reach Emprise."

Reprinted from Western Field and Stream, *St. Paul, Minn., December 1896.*

"Let me try, sir," urged the clerk. "I think I can make it, and I can't bear to see you suffer so. Think of your family, sir!"

A wrench of pain lined the trader's face. "Don't make it harder for me! If I live I shall not forget your generosity, Fred; but the odds are too great, you must not go."

He spoke in a low, wearied tone and burying his face in the robes again, dropped into an uneasy slumber. Stanson watched him silently for awhile, sitting by the fire. Then he turned to the men. "Gladieu; go and drive the horses in near the camp or they may drift with the storm. We might have to kill one yet. And you, Francois, cut plenty of wood and drag it up here; we'll soon be getting weak, without food, and the fire must not go out; that would be the end."

When they were gone Stanson rose quietly and got his snowshoes. He tied them on carefully and drew the belt about his waist in tighter, pulled the hood of his capot closely round his face and put on his fur mitts. Then catching up a rifle, with a parting glance back over his shoulder at his sleeping chief, he passed from the fire onto the wide white waste, into the lashing, smoking blizzard!

It was not more than nine in the morning, though no sun was to be seen. He ran on quickly for two hours, despite his long fast, and he was warmed and exhilarated by the exertion and the consciousness that he was striving in a good cause. The fine, sifting snow stung his face; the keen wind, which served to guide him, cut his side; yet he fought bravely on. Then he began to feel faint; he became chilled through, and had an almost overpowering desire to lie down and sleep. The wind was *so cold*; and the snow over which he staggered was so soft and white; it looked warm, he thought. Now he was dazed, and seemed to see lights, fires flash through the whirling flakes. Yet he was quite happy, and thought with pity of the poor trader and of the hungry men crouching over their camp fire.

Then he realized suddenly that his senses were flying and he halted short and glared into the swirl before him.

What was that?

He brushed his beaver mitt across his eyes to wipe away the rime and gazed hard in front.

That black thing?

Ah! he was dreaming no longer now—his senses were making a final rally. Here was food, shelter—life! It stood broadside to him, this thing, perfectly still, with its back to the storm and scarce twenty paces off. He was cool and collected now, though he had been flurried at first—standing with a frozen steel in his naked fingers, with capot thrown back and his clear blue eye looking steadily along the barrel. *Everything* rested on this aim. With a prayer in his heart, he pressed the trigger, the report rang out, and onto its knees, like a smitten ash, went—the great buffalo bull!

Only for an instant though. In the next he was up again and with a hoarse bellow of rage, rushing at his assailant. Stanson had pumped another cartridge into his gun, and awaited the onset fearlessly with it still pointed, until the shaggy foretop almost touched the muzzle. Then he pulled. Down dropped the huge brute, ploughing the snow and burying the legs of the clerk beneath him.

Stanson yelled with delight. Happily he was unhurt in the deep drift, though he had difficulty in withdrawing his feet. But he knew what to do then—he had heard a halfbreed tell. He slit the hide from the breast down with his heavy hunting knife, quickly removed the entrails and crawled inside. The back lay to the storm. He would get warm here; he would recruit his lost strength and then go on. He had travelled for a long time; it could not be much farther to the fort. He would save the trader yet.

He cut pieces from the carcass and ate them ravenously. Never had anyone before so enjoyed a feast. An hour had not gone when he was quite warm, and he felt fresh and invigorated. He drew himself out of his strange refuge and, re-tying his snowshoes, went on once more. No halting now. He sped over the snow, though the storm still raged, and long before darkness closed in, came out on the bank of Smoking River. He knew where he was then; it was only three miles to Fort Emprise, and at four o'clock exactly he walked into the trading shop.

"Send off fresh men with dogs to the trader at the bluff the other side of the Big Plain and tell Mrs. Regg to put in some of his asthma remedy. They're snowbound and starving, and he is bad with one of his attacks."

The clerk in charge looked at him in astonishment: "You don't mean to say—" but Stanson was gone. The dog train was despatched immediately and at ten o'clock that night the thankful trader and his men had relief. Stanson awoke next day just in time to welcome his chief on his arrival at one o'clock, safe and well. He grasped the hand of the young clerk and wrung it till tears stood in Stanson's eyes. There were tears, too, in the trader's eyes; though he did not speak.

"Stanson," said the trader one afternoon in the following spring, "I said I should not forget your brave act last winter. I recommended to the Commissioner and Council that you be advanced and I have just had word that you are promoted to senior clerk. That saves you your junior clerkship and if all goes well you are three years nearer a commission. I congratulate you."

It was a big jump for Stanson, and he felt elated. He was pleased at his promotion and the large increase in salary it meant, yet deep down in his heart was something that made him rejoice still more. He had long secretly admired the trader's daughter. Stanson was handsome, strong, active and a gentleman; young men of his stamp were few in this wild country. Small wonder, then, if Angela on her part had felt an attraction, scarcely realized, for him. Then his gallant rescue of her father filled her with gratitude. The gentle current of gratitude is often but an affluent of the deep stream of love on whose broad bosom these two young hearts were soon floating tranquilly together in the weeks that followed. They were happy in the present, in being all in all to one another and with the sun shining for them alone in the blue sky above.

But Stanson had thought of marriage—if, indeed, he had thought seriously of it at all—only as a remote possibility. He could not think of asking for her hand as a junior clerk. And Major Blume, commandant of the troop at Fort Emprise, who was a much greater man than poor Fred, was at no pains to cover his unqualified approval of Miss Angela as a very desirable young lady. True, she did not like him; he was a stout, middle-aged man with a drooping yellow moustache and a bass voice. But her father seemed to think highly of him—she might change.

But now everything was altered, and here was his opportunity. The trader still held his hand and, looking at him with kindly eyes, was asking if there was nothing else he could do while Stanson confusedly murmured his thanks and thought it all out.

"There is something—I wished to ask you," he said at length, hesitatingly, growing scarlet to the points of his ears. "I had not thought to do so now, though," he added quickly, "not for a long time, at least—but this makes a difference." He stopped a moment; then summoning all his courage, he looked straight at his chief and went on: "I love Angela, sir. Will you give her to me to be my wife?"

The trader dropped his hand and fell back a step as though he had received a blow between the eyes. He did not reply at once, and when he did, there was no kindness in the glance he turned upon Stanson.

"Have you spoken to her of this?"

"Yes;—and she is willing."

"It was very wrong in you, sir, an apprentice clerk, to make proposals to my daughter without my knowledge. Let me hear no more of this. I have other plans for her."

Mr. Trader Regg had made up his mind that no girl of his should wed a servant of the Company; no one less than a chief factor at all events. He had had his commission only eight years, though he had been thirty in the service, and he was yet very far from the rank of a chief factor. He did not realize that it is not circumstances, as a rule, that hold a man, that this young fellow had qualities which would carry him, probably, higher than he should ever attain to, before he had nearly the years of himself.

Stanson was crushed. What did his promotion count for now? It seemed to him that there was a tinge of irony in the trader's tones when he said to him next morning:

"Stanson, now that you are a full-fledged senior clerk, you must have more important work. I have decided to appoint you to the charge of Cleft Lake Post. You are young and energetic—just the man for the place. I expect the opposition will find you harder metal than McRob, who was there last winter. Be ready to leave tomorrow. You will have time to know your hunting Indians well enough to make advances with discretion in the fall. You can come up about the twentieth of September for your winter outfit."

Cleft Lake Post! Sixty miles away, through a wilderness of wood and stream and morass, and not a white man nearer than Fort Emprise. It was banishment—exile. But he could do nothing, but go. And go he did, but with a bitter, bitter feeling at his heart; his promotion had turned into a cup of gall for him.

It was the last day of September. Stanson had been at Fort Emprise a fortnight. He had managed to see Angela and she was still true to him. She had firmly persisted in her determination not to suffer any overtures from Major Blume; and though it was a sore disappointment to her father, he had apparently become resigned to the hopelessness of his cherished plan, for he cherished his daughter yet more dearly.

"Get your outfit together, Mr. Stanson," he said, in a more kindly tone than he had used towards him since the spring. "I am going with you, to inspect the posts; we will leave in the morning."

The trader was usually in a hurry about starting. In the past Fred had been accustomed to—"Now, Mr. Stanson, what's delaying you?"; Mr. Stanson this and Mr. Stanson that. But on this morning of the first of October he seemd to hang back. He loitered in the mess room, walking aimlessly around, gazing abstractedly at the floor and walls after everything was ready, while the others waited. At length he roused himself with apparent effort, as if shaking off a disagreeable feeling, and said briskly:

"We'll, as we're going, I supposed we'd best be off; it's just six."

Stanson got into the bow of the canoe with his dog Chips, the trader took his place in the centre and the steersman in the stern. At ten o'clock, aided by the strong current, they had made thirty miles and put ashore at the head of a small island over which led a portage, for the river was like a mill-race on either side. Just below were the Seething Falls—a long, turbulent rapid. They put the canoe into the eddy wheeling slowly at the foot of the island and pushed off. It was necessary to strike into the channel on the right, keeping the bow of the boat well up, and paddle hard for the slack water along the opposite shore—but the steersman must have been at fault. The frail bark shot half into the surge, stopped, trembled an instant—then it was riding away, bottom up, and three human beings were battling fiercely for life in the angry flow of Smoking River.

The Indian steersman had been thrown partly within the eddy and he struck at once back for the island. The broad, deep streams which feed the Arctic seas are not warm, even in mid-summer, and this was October; yet he reached it in safety. When his feet touched, he turned. The hands of the two white men were linked across the bottom of the canoe; he could hear Stanson entreating the trader (who was a large, unwieldy man and unable to swim) to be calm. As the canoe swept around a bend at the head of the falls in the distance, the hands parted—a splash!—then the Indian saw only the ceaseless river, a symbol of time, flowing swiftly on between its silent, wooded shores.

A York boat's crew was working up Seething Falls on its way from Hudson Bay to Fort Emprise. A spaniel ran to the shore opposite, sat down and set out a piteous howl. The bowsman looked, with the pole poised in his hand, and exclaimed:

"Why, if there ain't Fred Stanson's dog!"

"Looks like him," agreed the guide. "Wonder what he's doin' here?"

"Fred ought to be on the way down to his post 'bout now. Maybe the dog's followed 'long shore an' got lost."

"Put in, men!" ordered the guide. "We'll take him on. Fred thinks more o' that pup than a silver fox."

They poled for the little bay and round a point came on an upturned canoe.

"Why, what's this?"

A body floated beside it, tied by the wrist to the painter. It was Trader Regg. They scarcely needed to be told by the Indian, whom they picked up at the island, how it had happened.

Christmas Eve at Fort Emprise, and from the white mud chimneys at the points of the solid, square-roofed buildings light columns of smoke drift slowly up into the frosty air, while the weest star above twinkles frantically, as though afraid it should escape notice from the sons of men on this great night of halleluiahs. In the north the aurora borealis shoots forth gorgeous scintillating panels of pink and green and scarlet and lemon to the zenith with a gentle rustling, until the wintry landscape glows beneath it almost as bright as day. The thick armor upon the bosom of the great lake before the old fort booms sullenly under the silent rending might of the frost king, and the caves below give back rumbling echoes, growing faint and still more faint as the rift cleaves out toward the centre. A dark background of firs partially encircles the fort and under their quiet shadows at one point nestles a little plot with a white paling about it, inside which the officers and servants of the Honourable Governor and Company of Adventurers of England trading into Hudson's Bay have one by one been laid to rest any time these two hundred years. The last to join that silent group is Trader Regg, and a soft drapery of pure white covers the unbeautiful mound of bare earth, over which grass will grow in the spring.

The fort buildings are ablaze with light. To and fro across the square flit hurrying figures, the walks answering to their steps with a crisp, ringing sound not to be mistaken.

"Whut's all the scurry, boy?" asks a grizzled, shaggy giant with black eyes and hair and the roll of his tongue like a snare drum on the word "scurry." It is John Slack, oldest of the boat guides, who had a Scotsman for a father and a Saulteaux woman for a mother; he has just come over from the servants' quarters to buy "his girl" a Christmas present of a pair of "English shoes." "Whut's to do? Muny a Yul'-tide have I seen at this aul' foort, but no'er a wan t' appro'ch the like o' thus fer acteevity. It's extr'ordinar', boy; extr'ordinar', whatever."

The man addressed is sixty if a day and like his interrogator is of mixed blood, though the half of him that is white is French instead of Orkneyan. He pauses a moment with a look akin to awe upon his swarthy features.

"Boy!" he ejaculates in a dramatic whisper, "de Commissionaire been come!" Then he hurries on. Had His Majesty the Czar of all the Russias happened in at Emprise, the incident would, perhaps, have occasioned only a mild degree of wonder or curiosity with the majority of its populace. But the arrival of the Commissioner of the whole Hudson's Bay Company at one of the two hundred posts under his supervision—that was an event! And the Commissioner and Christmas both hitting the post on the same night! It was something to place as a landmark in the history of the country alongside the Small Pox Year.

But a yet greater surprise is in store for them on this long-to-be-remembered night, though that may well seem impossible. There is a lively tinkle of sleigh bells down the road leading through the firs and cries of "Eul! Eul!"—"Jah! Jah!" and before the group in front of the trading shop has time to speculate on what is approaching, five great Huskie dogs come bounding through the big gate of the stockade with a low carriole swinging at their heels and pull up short, panting furiously, in the middle of the square.

"Drive to the *waskiagan* of Okema Regg," says a manly voice from among the furs which appear to fill the sleigh, and they turn off to a large house on the right less brilliantly lighted than the others and which bears about it an indefinite air of sombreness. Here a young man—with the help of one of the Indian drivers for he is benumbed with cold—rises and, stepping stiffly out of the carriole, walks to the door and knocks. A tall girl, dressed in deep black and with the shadow of a great sorrow upon her beautiful face, through which there yet shines the sanctity of a chastened resignation, opens it. She starts back with a stifled cry and places her hands over her heart, while a wild look comes into her eyes and her face grows deadly pale. The stranger takes a step forward into the light and stretches forth his hands. Then with a little scream and the one word—"Fred!" she falls swooning into his arms.

He carries her to a couch and sits down, still with his arms about her, and kisses her over and over on the lips. Presently she opens her eyes.

"Oh, Fred," she says, "you have come back to me—from the dead! Speak—speak to me—tell me that it is so! Oh! I cannot believe it! Say that it is not a horrid nightmare!"

"I have come back to you indeed," he says, fondly looking down into her eyes. "I have come back to you, in the flesh."

"But how—how did you escape? And why did you not return to us at once? We thought that you were drowned with—with him." She speaks the last word softly.

"I did not know. It was my dog, my brave little Chips—he must have pulled me out, unconscious. It was not far and the water was slack; perhaps I struggled and so helped him. I tried to save—him; tied his wrist to the painter of the canoe. Then, I believe, I sank. And—and that is all I remember; it was all a blur. When I came to myself I was alone, in the depth of the forest, lost and starving. I wandered then, for another day—ah, it was awful!—and then reason in mercy left me again. An Indian hunter, making the round of his traps fell upon my trail. He followed it and found me dying at the foot of a tree. I had roamed aimlessly more than a hundred miles from the scene of the accident, and this was either the sixth or eighth day since it had occurred—but you know I was very strong. All this I learned afterward; for six weeks I lay delirious with fever in the hunters' camp, whither my rescuer had borne me, bound tightly so that I could not move. When the crisis was past, they carried me—the faithful fellows—to Cleft Lake, the nearest post, where I rapidly gained strength and learned that my brave dog was safe here at Emprise. I must have scared him from me when I was wandering, a madman, in those dreadful woods. And—that is all."

There is another knock at the door. The news of Stanson's arrival has swept through the fort and the Commissioner himself is the first to call upon him. Without waiting for an answer to his rap, he walks in.

"Pardon me," he says, coming forward somewhat hesitatingly and with a slight air of embarrassment. "My dear young fellow, my impatience to grasp the hand of a noble friend and a faithful officer—for officer you are from this day—must be my apology for this, I fear, not altogether fortunate—or shall I say wel-come?"—he glances smilingly at the conscious Angela—"intrusion. I have heard your story and you are wearied with your long day, so I shall not ask you to repeat it until you have had a good night's rest."

Just then the door opens and Stanson's short, sturdily built little dog, frantic with delight and barking and whining incessantly by turns, tumbles over himself in his eagerness to reach his master, upon whom he leaps with every demonstration of affection and joy that an animal is capable of showing. Stanson lifts him in his arms and presses his face into the soft silken fur of his neck.

"Ah, Chips!" he says tremulously while his eyes grow moist, "my brave little brute, are you glad to see me? How did you ever do it? You will be more to me than ever now."

Mrs. Regg and her younger daughters, returning from a round of charitable visits among the destitute in the Indian camp, had given the dog the opportunity to slip in. Like everybody else, they had heard some details of Stanson's rescue and now they come forward, deeply moved by feelings of mingled joy and sorrow, to press his hand. Next the clerks come, with a wealth of right glad welcome, and tears which they fight manfully though with ill-success to keep back or hide; and after them the servants and labourers.

Just before the Christmas dinner next day an interesting ceremony, which is witnessed by the whole population of Fort Emprise, including Major Blume, takes place at the home of the Reggs. It is conducted by the Commissioner, and at its close he says:

"Gentlemen, fill your glasses and drink to the health and happiness of the bride and of her gallant husband—who in her, by the help of God, has just received the Christmas gift of his life—Chief Trader Stanson, commissioned officer in charge of Lake Chincho District, with headquarters at Fort Emprise."

And Chips, who from his seat hard by on the carpet has been intently watching his master's face during the ceremony, here sets up a tremendous barking and so gives his unreserved endorsement to the entire proceedings.

In October of 1892 the author's best friend Stanley Simpson—Fred Stanson in the story—drowned while attempting to save the life of his Chief Factor in the icy "white water" of the Nelson River. The factor was Horace Belanger.

Christmas at Fort Pitt

Christmas was coming to old Fort Pitt on the North Saskatchewan, still in that year of 1884 an outpost of the white man's civilization, and preparations were afoot to celebrate in becoming manner, according to custom, that time-honoured festival of peace on earth, good will toward men.

Otto Dufresne, the white-haired diminutive French-Canadian "Company" cook ("The Little Oak" to the Crees because of his remarkable strength), had outdone himself. Under the supervision of beloved and motherly Mrs. McLean, the chief trader's wife, and her three comely daughters, he had prepared delicious wild rice soup, roast young beaver, tender and succulent as lamb, which it much resembled; roast prairie chicken and partridge, berry pemmican, pies, cakes and of course the one item lacking which no Christmas dinner could be complete—a royal plum pudding with brandy sauce.

Then there were the decorations. The walls of the dining-room were draped in white and navy blue, with sprays and festoons of spruce intertwining cross arms of muskets and revolvers; four wreaths of spruce enclosing the symbols "H.B.C.," "N.W.M.P.," "I.D." (Indian Department) and "Our Guests," worked in scarlet monograms; and on a background of the Union Jack and the Hudson's Bay Company flag, in white lettering, the words "Welcome," "Merry Christmas" and "Happy New Year." In place of the unobtainable holly, there were cranberries *au branche* from the neighbouring muskeg. Not even the mistletoe had been forgotten, bunched clippings of Saskatoon twigs replacing that osculatory indispensable. A large star of fir over the centre of the room completed a list of decorations at once pleasing, tasteful and characteristic of the season and the country.

Reprinted from The Beaver, *Winnipeg, Man., December 1945.*

The glorious day opened with the established all-round Christmas greetings among the members of the isolated little community and calls by the personnel of the North-West Mounted Police detachment, who were quartered in Company buildings, on Chief Trader W. J. McLean and his numerous family. Then there were gifts to the little ones of the brood from individual friends among the police. Everybody and his wife received a welcoming handshake and a serving of the refreshments provided by the Company's head in "The Big House."

Following breakfast, Stanley Simpson, the Company's accountant at the fort, was tying on his snowshoes preparatory to making the round of his trapline, lying along the towering hills overlooking Pitt across the river, and of course I needed no invitation to join him. Climbing the steep banks to the heights above, a mile or two to the east, we reached the first trap, which we found had not been disturbed. Two miles farther on we took from the second trap a prime red fox and before reaching the end of the line we picked up two more, one red, the other a finely marked cross fox. So Stanley's trap line was paying dividends. (I should make it plain that in some districts the officer in charge encouraged the employees to set out traplines in their spare time and so add to their wages as well as to the yearly returns of the district itself, for of course their catches of fur were always sold to the Company.)

Stanley led the whole seven-mile run. He was a strong athletic young fellow of about my own age, tireless and fast afoot. At the annual sports day at Battleford the previous summer he had been matched to race a halfbreed called "Northwest" who held the N.W.T. record for the distance in the three-quarter-mile event. Coming into the home stretch Simpson, who was trailing his opponent, stumbled and fell full length to the ground, and there were groans of dismay from his partisans who at once concluded that the race was over. But Simpson was on his feet like a flash and in a burst of speed that brought cheer on cheer from the sidelines he overhauled and passed the halfbreed and romped across the tape a winner.

Stanley also had an amazingly strong grip. He was the only man I ever knew who could place a double-spring beaver trap on his knee and set it, using his hands alone. Ordinarily a trapper placed the trap on the ground and pressed the springs down either side by standing on them; then bending over to raise the pan and set it.

We arrived back at the fort just in time to shed our snowshoes and make ourselves presentable before joining the big Company family and its guests at the Christmas dinner. One of the guests at the table, I should mention, was Captain Francis Dickens, son of the novelist, in command of the Fort Pitt detachment, NWMP, in which he held the rank of inspector.

Dinner over, we adjourned to the office, where Manila cheroots—an article of commerce at that date imported and stocked by the Hudson's Bay Company—were passed around by our host.

Then, "according to plan," we divided into two competing groups for the rabbit hunt, which was an important feature of the day's programme. One party was headed by the chief trader, the other—if memory serves me—by Angus McKay. All the grown-ups in the large McLean family, including the three eldest girls, "shouldered arms" like veteran troopers and marched forth to "The Battle of the Bunnies." I cannot recall which side got the larger number but I know we had a lot of fun, snowballing and racing, while not overlooking the main object of potting the prey.

I may explain that every so often in the park-like north country, the rabbits become very numerous and then suddenly die off, so that few are left in the following year to carry on production. But they soon again begin to multiply and start another cycle of mounting increases. This must have been the peak year of one of these cycles, for I never saw rabbits more plentiful, and the red willow everywhere was stripped of its bark for a height of two feet or more above the snow.

In those short December days the sun "went out," as the Indians say, early, and it was nearly nightfall when we called off the contest and returned to the fort and another sumptuous meal. After we had satisfied our appetites, which had razor-like edges following our tramp and frolics in the biting winter air, and had enjoyed more cheroots in the office, we returned to the reception room in the Big House and played "Post Office," "Pass the Button," and other games or cards, sang songs and thrummed guitars and the piano, to round out a day crammed full of merry-making and excitement. Then it was off to bed, another active and joyful Christmas at Fort Pitt to live long in our memory.

Adventurers All

The Fur Trade in the Far North

Pro pelle cutem—"Skin for skin." This is the motto of the oldest and greatest fur trading corporation in the world, with the liberal translation of it common throughout the country over which its operations extend. Within the vast area included between the Arctic Ocean and Alaska on the north and the forty-ninth parallel of latitude and the Great Lakes on the south, and the east coast of Labrador and the Pacific, the Hudson's Bay Company has two hundred trading posts and employs two thousand men in the business of collecting and exporting furs. A short description of its methods, the life of its employees and hunters and of the territory over which, for upward of two centuries, it held almost undisputed sway, should embrace nearly everything worthy of mention relative to the fur trade in the Far North.

The chief executive officer of the company in Canada is called the commissioner, and he resides at Winnipeg, where the head offices are also located. The territory is divided by the company, for its own purposes, into four departments comprising thirty districts, each under the supervision of a commissioned officer; and the number of posts to a district varies from three to ten.

A commissioned officer originally shared in the profits of the fur trade, a commission representing a given number of shares according to the rank of the officer. Of these there were five: chief factors, factors, chief traders, traders, and accountants. Recently, however, this system has been superseded by a scale of fixed salaries ranging from one thousand to two thousand five hundred dollars a year. Clerks and postmasters receive twenty to one hundred pounds sterling ($100 to $500) per annum, while the pay of labourers is proportionally less. These salaries, it is true, are not

Reprinted from The Northwest, *St. Paul, Minnesota, February 1897.*

large; yet, when it is understood that all employees live at the Company's expense, that they can purchase what goods they require for their own use at actual cost, and that many of them are able, during a long term of service, with modest sums which they have saved accumulating for years at compound interest, to educate their families at the best schools and universities and put away sufficient to keep them if not in affluence at least in comfort after retirement, it will scarcely seem a matter for wonder that they are as a rule content; that they are loyal to the interests they serve; and that many of the old servants and pensioners retain more affection for "the Company" than they profess regard for the government, and resign the active battle of life satisfied that they have acquitted themselves creditably and are entitled to a well-earned rest and such quiet pleasures as may be within their reach.

The capital stock invested in the fur trade (1897) is, in round numbers, four million dollars in shares of twenty pounds sterling each. This is exclusive of the land and other stock, which amounts to about six million dollars. The proceeds from the fur sales in a recent year were a million and a quarter of dollars, and the net profit on the season's trade, to be divided among the shareholders, was about three hundred thousand dollars.

It is, however, more particularly with the details of life in the remote portions of what may still be termed the Hudson's Bay Territory, and with the methods of taking, preparing and exporting the peltries which go to adorn the persons and equipages of the potentates of the civilized world, that it is here proposed to deal.

A "skin" was formerly the common unit of value in the fur trade, and it is still the specie of the Far North. It is represented by a bit of wood, called a "made beaver." A cotton handkerchief costs a skin, a pound of tea two, and a trade gun twenty; a mink is worth one, a beaver four, and a silver fox twenty skins. It is impossible to place a definite value upon the made-beaver skin, for it may be said to stand for anything from fifty cents to a dollar and a half, according to circumstances.

About the beginning of October the Indian hunter comes to the nearest Company's post. He is told that his debt is already, perhaps, fifty or sixty skins, for he has to live during the summer, when no furs are to be taken, and the company has given him advances. He haggles about the amount of further debt he is to obtain, for he is prepared to accept all he can get; by the time he leaves for his hunting grounds, his account probably reaches one hundred skins. It is safe to say that he will have at least half a sack of flour, a plug or two of tobacco, five pounds of tea, ten pounds of bacon, ammunition, a butcher and a pocketknife, an awl, some embroidery silk, a gaudy shawl, eight yards of pink or lilac print, steel traps and some confectionery. He has also, probably a little sugar, and perhaps some syrup, a cotton shirt and a blanket capote.

Arrived at his hunting ground, his first care is to select his camp, usually on the shore of some lake, and build a rough hut of logs and bark. If there be wild rice at hand, he gathers a sack or two, paddling along the reed-like stalks and threshing the heads between sticks so that the ripe grain falls into the canoe. So soon as the first snow comes, he endeavors to secure a store of meat. He is sure to have a partner, and two Indians not infrequently slay thirty or forty deer in a single hunt. The deer move about in droves and in different winters are found usually in different localities so that it is not always easy for the hunter to obtain a supply of venison.

These preliminary steps taken, the hunter goes about the work of laying his traps. He sets a line of them fifteen or twenty miles in circumference, so that the first and last traps are nearest his camp. Some are for bears—snares, made of rope, usually; others, for skunks, martens, fishers and wolverines, are the ordinary "figure-four" wooden deadfalls; beavers, otters, mink, foxes and wolves are taken in steel traps, while lynx are caught in twine snares.

It may take the hunter several days to make the round of his traps. A blanket, gun, knife, flint and steel, kettle, ax, snowshoes and a little tea and tobacco compose his equipment; when night falls he sets snares for rabbits, builds a shelter of boughs, and after a hearty meal of lynx, beaver, porcupine, skunk or bear, washed down by generous draughts of strong black tea from his copper pail, followed by a pipe, he lays himself down beside his lonely campfire, wrapped in his single blanket, under the cold, glistening stars and the scintillating glory of the Northern Lights, to doze and shiver until dawn.

Everything is fish that comes to his net, and the flesh of any of the animals named, as well as of other fur-robed quadrupeds, is eaten by him with relish. Beaver is excellent, as I am myself able to testify; so is lynx—notwithstanding its relation to the feline tribe—and muskrat. The rest do not rank quite so high in his estimation.

So soon as the ice takes on the lakes and rivers, or about the middle of November, a dog train or two is dispatched from the trading post with fresh supplies of flour, bacon, tea, tobacco and ammunition for the hunters, and to bring back their furs. A clerk is sent in charge and he is accompanied by an Indian or halfbreed guide, who is also an interpreter should the clerk be ignorant of the native language. Such a trip may occupy four to ten days and generally results in several hundreds of dollars' worth of furs being brought back to be placed to the credit of the hunters' accounts at the fort.

Perhaps it is here that the dog attains his highest sphere of usefulness. Four is the usual number allotted to a "train." They are harnessed, one before the other, to a "flatsled" which carries the goods and the men's provisions, besides fish for the dogs. The men run most of the time, one on snowshoes before the dogs, the other behind, and from twenty to fifty miles is an ordinary day's journey. Sixty miles, indeed, is not an uncommon record between sunrise and sunset on a broken trail—a record from which some idea of the training and endurance of the dog drivers may be gained.

The dogs are fed but once a day—at night; to feed them in the morning, say the drivers, makes them lazy. They are large, thick-haired animals, with pointed ears, small eyes and a generally wolfish appearance, and they are incorrigible thieves. Their hardiness may be understood when it is mentioned that, with the thermometer at fifty or sixty degrees below zero, they will rest, curled up in the snow, throughout the night. Were the commonly accepted superstition respecting the ill omen of a dog's howl to obtain in the fur country, people would dwell in perpetual horror of impending disaster, for a night never passes without a chorus from the dogs, lasting ten or fifteen minutes. In extreme cold weather I have often fancied that they howled to start the blood circulating and keep themselves warm; while in summer there is no doubt that the exercise of their vocal genius is often due to exasperation caused by the attacks of swarms of mosquitoes.

A few days before Christmas the hunters come in for the holidays and a period of feasting ensues. After the holidays the Indians return to their hunting grounds, but as fur animals do not move about much during the extreme cold, the furs they take are usually few during January and February. About the first of March they are once more at the fort for their outfit for the spring hunt. This lasts until well on toward the end of June, and is the Indian's harvest. Fur is at its best, the days are long and pleasant, and it is spring!—that season so full of hope and promise for all. About the first of May, or as soon as the ice in the rivers breaks up, supplies are sent as in the fall to the Indian camps, though they go this time in canoes instead of by sled. They are in the charge of a clerk and bring back the furs which the hunters have, up to then, succeeded in taking. This tripping is frequently attended with more or less danger, on account of rapids and falls, in which many a man has lost his life.

The quantity and value of the furs which an Indian may secure as the result of his spring hunt varies greatly, of course, but in a good year from two to three hundred dollars' worth may be taken as a fair average. He may have eight or ten bears, a dozen beavers, four or five otters, a number of lynx, martens and mink and several hundred musquash or muskrats. When all the hunters have come in, the furs are pressed into packs of a hundred pounds each and sent in York boats to the frontier trails, over which they are carted to the nearest railway station to be shipped to London, England, where they are carefully sorted and afterward sold at the two great annual sales of the Company in January and March, which are attended by buyers from all parts of the world.

In the hard life of the voyageur there is ever present the elements of danger and excitement. With the first glance of dawn, the guide shouts his warning *"Leve! Leve!"* and the men spring from their blankets, pack their camp outfit into the boats, and are off. Six oars go to a boat, one to a man, besides a "sweep" in the hands of both bow and steersman. The oars are large and heavy, and the rowers rise to their feet and sink back into their seats with each long stroke. At eight o'clock they put ashore for breakfast, and about noon another halt is made; then they go on until night falls, when they stop for the day, eat their supper and throw themselves on the ground for a few hours' rest. I have been told by voyageurs that they have been so tired at night that they were unable to eat and have flung themselves down on the nearest level spot without so much as removing their coats or snatching a blanket, and slept the sleep of dead weariness until roused at daybreak by the cry of the guide.

Fifteen to twenty miles is, perhaps, an average day's journey; much depends upon the water. In some places, rapids and portages occur with exasperating frequency; in others the stream is broad and deep and there is little current. Again, in crossing a lake, with a favourable wind, sail may be made and the rowers have a welcome rest. While in breasting a rapid, round which it is unnecessary or impossible to portage, "tracking" is resorted to. A long line is attached to the bow of the boat and the men disembark, leaving only the bow and steersman to keep her nose off the shore or off rocks in the stream, while the men far ahead on the bank haul her up against the torrent.

Accidents are common. A block of overhanging ice, four or five feet thick and left by the spring flood, may fall upon a man as he passes beneath it and crush out his life; a sudden access of force in the current, as the boat rounds a bend, may jerk the trackers from their feet and into the river, and some may not get out again; or the boat may drift against a rock, smash to atoms, and the cargo and the men in her be lost.

But portaging is the hardest work which comes to the voyageur; for, sometimes, it is necessary to drag the heavy York boat and to carry her load of four or five tons over a rough, rocky point a mile in width. A portage strap is fastened to one "piece" of about one hundred pounds; another piece, or perhaps two, is placed upon this, and with the strap against his forehead, with bared legs and shoeless feet, man after man toils across the portage, until the narrow path beneath him is damp with the sweat which rolls from his body.

In former times, buffalo pemmican constituted the chief food of the voyageur; now dried moose or cariboo has taken its place. Then, tea and flour were luxuries enjoyed but once a year, at Christmas; now they form part of his daily ration.

As may be imagined, the life of a Company's officer or clerk does not possess much novelty. If the clerk is fortunate enough to be stationed at the district headquarters, he may perhaps live at the same table with his commissioned officer and his family; there may be young ladies, in which event music and cards help to while away the long winter evenings. There is also a library of greater or less dimensions; and if he be of a literary turn, magazines and papers reach him as often as twice to twelve times a year, as he may be near or far from the arteries of the great outside world. In any event, the arrivals of the mails form, perhaps, the most notable breaks in the monotonous life, bringing tidings of home and friends and of those things of which he was once a part and which linger ever in his heart and memory, no matter how long it may have been since he bade farewell to them all. Dances, too, assist in killing time, and if the occasion be a wedding, a dance is likely to last for two or three days, for leisure is usually abundant in this great, quiet land.

But hunting is the main recreation of the majority of the officers and clerks. The staff at a post often go out and camp for a week, and a hundred or more geese and double that number of ducks, load their boats on the return. The ptarmigan—brown in summer and white in winter—is a good game bird, and in some localities pinnated grouse or prairie chickens are very numerous. Our spruce little friend, the partridge, too, is nowhere more frequently at home to the hunter than here, and he is often such a stranger to the guile of man that an Indian will walk up to the tree upon which he is sitting and slip the noose that he has fixed to the end of a pole over his head.

After the first snow in the fall, rabbit shooting is good sport and, in seasons when they are plentiful, fifty or sixty to the credit of a single huntsman in an afternoon is not an uncommon score. Then there is the large game, such as moose and deer, while now and then a bear, in his simplicity, pokes his nose in inquisitive proximity to the fort, the staff turn out, and he is shot for his trouble.

At one of the posts where I was stationed, we kept a moose for two years. She was taken when very young by an Indian who killed her mother and brought the calf to the fort in his canoe. She became quite tame and in the second winter we broke her to drive in harness. Her chief amusements were scaring Indians by racing up to them, stopping abruptly with a loud snort, and planting her forefeet on the backs of the train dogs. A train dog will howl upon the slightest excuse and the pathetic outbursts called forth by the successful performance of this latter feat appeared to cause "Maud" unstinted enjoyment and a certain amount of wonder which was ludicrous to behold.

The clerks often set traps adjacent to the fort, and in this way find another means of passing time and of adding to their incomes. Snowshoeing is also popular exercise on the short days, and, at posts where they are kept, horses are in much demand.

At an outpost where a clerk is alone with his Indian servant, however, the life is wearisome to a degree and privation not infrequently adds to the hardship of it. Supplies may run short and in any case he is expected to stock himself with fish for his table and his dogs, taken in nets from the lake near which his post is situated, as well as to augment his larder by the use of his gun. Rare instances have occurred where, through accident, supplies had not reached the far out posts for which they were intended, and the men had literally died of starvation.

Out of a York boat's crew which was taking the annual supplies for a post far up among the Rockies on a branch of the Mackenzie River, two or three men were drowned and, the ice beginning to take, the boat was obliged to put back to the district headquarters. The three men at the outpost were left for some weeks without the supplies and not until after winter had set in did it become possible to reach them with dog trains. When provisions were at length sent them, two were found dead in the post, while the third man was living by himself in a small hut some distance from the fort buildings.

The explanation he gave was that he had removed to where there was a chance of keeping himself alive by snaring rabbits, which were more plentiful than at the post, but a suggestion of cannibalism pervaded the affair, for only the bones of his companions were found, and they were in the open chimney place. Nothing was done, however, and I myself saw the survivor many times in after years, though I never spoke to him of that winter. One of the two men who went to the relief told me of the circumstances.

The prices paid to the hunters for their furs at the present time are, of course, much higher than they were fifty years ago. In London a beaver was worth four to ten and a silver fox fifty to three hundred dollars. Tea, tobacco and powder are now (1897) sold at a dollar a pound, and shot, sugar and bacon bring fifty, and flour twenty cents per pound in the Far North. But in the days when an ordinary colored cotton handkerchief paid for a marten skin, the value of which was three dollars, they could rarely—with the exception of tobacco and ammunition—be had at any price, and dry goods, being lightest, formed the bulk of the Company's yearly outfit. For the cost of getting merchandise into that almost inaccessible region was very great, and it should not be forgotten that, though the Company assuredly made enormous profits, it treated the Indians, on the whole, humanely. Fur was plentiful and a good hunter could always pay his debt, even though it might be large, if he tried. The Company was ready to advance him at all times and, in sickness or starvation, it came to his aid.

Of late years, the Hudson's Bay territory, even in the most remote parts, as the Yukon, the Mackenzie and northern British Columbia, has been invaded by the "free" traders—to their profit and the discomfiture of the ancient order. Now steamboats, owned by the Company and the missions, ply on the Athabasca, Peace and Mackenzie rivers; tourists have visited and written of it, and the "Great Lone Land" is no more the *terra incognita* that it once was. Gold and other precious minerals are abundant, as are coal, petroleum, and various natural products. Potatoes and other roots, and even wheat and barley, are grown in the more favored districts; while whitefish, pike, pickerel, trout, sturgeon and salmon abound in the larger lakes and streams. Large quantities of whitefish are caught with nets in the fall and frozen for food for men and dogs during the winter. At York Factory and other points on Hudson Bay, wild geese are so numerous, before the ice takes, that they are salted and issued as rations to the servants—who are said, by the way, to grow excessively tired of them.

A ship still comes annually to York and Moose factories on Hudson Bay, from London, England, but the bulk of the fur now goes out by Montreal or New York, while most of the supplies are bought in Canada and the United States. Formerly, all goods were English goods, and the furs were all exported by ship from Hudson Bay—by which route, also, the servants and officers of the Company, going or returning, had passage.

Furs are not now so plentiful as in the olden times, yet they are by no means exhausted, and the Company discourages the slaughter of fur bearing animals out of season. The following table, which is authentic, shows the quantities of the different varieties of furs sold by the Company in two recent years.

Description	Average Value	Number of Skins		Amounts	
		1887	1894	1887	1894
Bear	$18.00	8,087	9,173	$145,566	$165,144
Beaver	5.00	83,589	46,779	417,945	233,895
Fishers	7.50	4,492	4,024	33,888	30,180
Foxes, blue	5.00	35	34	175	170
Foxes, cross	7.50	3,185	2,970	23,888	22,275
Foxes, red	1.75	11,651	15,810	20,389	27,668
Foxes, silver	75.00	827	04	62,025	45,300
Foxes, white	3.00	4,102	3,227	12,306	9,681
Lynx	3.50	73,850	12,813	258,475	44,845
Marten	3.50	50,842	108,997	177,947	381,490
Mink	2.00	64,215	51,163	128,430	102,326
Musquash	.10	380,000	648,000	38,000	64,800
Otters, land	8.00	8,312	7,444	66,496	59,552
Otters, sea	15.00	10	11	150	165
Seals, fur	12.00	1,846	44,086	22,152	529,032
Skunks	.75	10,920	6,785	8,190	5,089
Wolves	1.50	1,136	2,037	1,704	3,055
Wolverines	4.50	1,226	880	5,517	3,960

Totals $1,423,045 $1,728,597

The above values are, of course, only approximate, and in some instances may be somewhat too high; but the figures may be taken as a reasonable estimate. The prices of first quality furs are in most cases much higher than those quoted, but the number of inferior skins reduces the average values. The highest price of which I have heard as being paid for a silver fox, for example, was one hundred and five pounds sterling, or five hundred and eleven dollars. A good otter is worth ten to fifteen dollars and a beaver eight to ten, at any time. The numbers of peltries mentioned represent, perhaps, nine-tenths of the total catch in the Hudson's

Bay territory for the respective years, for it is the policy of the Company to control the London market, and almost all those furs gathered by the free traders find their way, by purchase, into the Company's hands before they leave America.

In conclusion, it may be said that the fur trade life is not without its attractions, especially to the young. R. M. Ballantyne, the well known author whose tales of adventure have been the delight of thousands of boys, began life as a clerk in the service of the Hudson's Bay Company. The freedom, the outdoor sports, the wildness and novelty of his surroundings and a certain glamour of romance—all tend to act upon the impressionable heart of youth. It is, moreover, essentially a home life. Thus, when the novelty and enthusiasm have worn off and he has become one with it, with ties, perhaps, of family, with his modest pay slowly mounting up to a competency for his old age, it will scarcely be thought surprising that the employee of the Company, once in the service, usually spends the active part of his life in it, his twilight years in the country, and is buried in the land of his adoption.

Since 1670, two hundred years before the arrival of the North-West Mounted Police in the West, the Hudson's Bay Company had been in intimate touch with the Indians. They had come not as conquerors, but as peaceful traders, whose chief purpose was to collect as many furs as possible. They discouraged intertribal wars, which ruined trade, and cultivated the trust and friendship of the Indians. Aside from any altruistic considerations, this was good business. The Company was no fly-by-night, anxious to make quick profits and then retire, as did many of the independent traders and the North West Company partners. It was in the country to stay and the Indian trapper was a vital part of its business, for without the native hunters and trappers there would have been little fur to trade. The welfare and efficiency of the Indian was thus of the utmost importance to the trader. How well the Company men succeeded in establishing friendly relations with the tribes may be judged from the words of the first lieutenant-governor of Manitoba: "The Indians of Canada have, owing to the manner in which they were dealt with for generations by the Hudson's Bay Company, an abiding confidence in the Government of the Queen."

There was another factor, too, which contributed materially to the good feeling that prevailed between the Company's traders and the Indians. In the very early days white women, except in rare instances, were virtually unknown in Rupert's Land, as the country was then designated, and many of the Company's men, officers included, took Indian wives, chiefly from the tribes of

Algonquin stock—Cree and Saulteaux. As a result, a considerable population of families of mixed Scotch, English, French and Indian blood came into being. Many of the offspring of these marriages were sent in the Company's ships to Great Britain and the continent to be educated and, returning, entered the Company's service also. Thus a bond of blood and amicable relationship was established between the Indians and their descendants and the Company personnel, and the red men came to look to the men of the old organization for information and advice. In passing, it may be mentioned that a large number of the men and women owing their existence to these unions came to occupy distinguished positions in the public life of the Dominion.

The Company officers, of course, had advance notice about the coming to the West of the North-West Mounted Police, and after the Indians also learned of the impending invasion they sought counsel of their friends, "the trading men." As a consequence they were prepared to accept the intrusion as designed largely for their benefit, and to welcome the newcomers. Slaughtered ruthlessly for their robes by "skin hunters" from south of the line armed with long-range repeating rifles, the buffalo were rapidly disappearing, and with their disappearance went the chief source of livelihood of the majority of the red peoples on the plains.

The way was thus smoothed for the Canadian Government, aided by officials of the Company, to negotiate treaties whereby the tribes relinquished their inherent rights in the domain of their forefathers and accepted in return provision for their sustenance and further wellbeing. Thus in no small measure the Company was responsible for removing any obstacle to the flood of white settlers presently pouring into the West, and peaceful colonization of the country was made possible.

The Rum Trade

It used to be said that civilization's first two gifts to the savage were the Bible and the bottle, that to whatever remote quarter of the globe he might fare, the white man carried with him to its primitive inhabitant in one hand the means of salvation for his soul and in the other the agent for the damnation of his body.

We know that, as applied to North America at least, this saying is largely true. The trader and the missionary usually arrived together. The aim of the missionary was unselfish; he came preaching the doctrine of redemption. The purpose of the trader, on the contrary, was apt to be entirely selfish; he came to make money and the welfare, spiritual or otherwise, of the wild people with whom he dealt concerned him little.

There were, of course, exceptions. One was the Hudson's Bay Company, whose officers generally were humane men, but in the main this was the unlovely fact. And the trader quickly learned which among his wares was most prized. The red man, his appetite once whetted, would barter the last thing he possessed for a dram of the white man's magic potion, the fiery liquid which in a twinkling took him out of himself and into a new world, a world of riotous abundance, of unnumbered wives, of unlimited food, while at the same time he was transformed into a warrior so brave, holding fear in such contempt, that he might call on the very Muche Manitou, the Devil himself, to come forth and fight him.

The narratives left by the early traders afford an illuminating picture of the liquor traffic and its demoralizing effects upon the savages. Though long since abolished, until the middle of the last century this traffic endured as an established institution. On almost every page of the journal of Alexander Henry the Younger,

Manuscript in the Cameron Papers.

for example, may be found some allusion to the trade in liquor and its sinister results. Henry was a keen observer and a painstaking recorder; he has left a most graphic and comprehensive view of the fur trade life of his day. In 1800 he was the officer of the North West Company in charge of a post or district on the upper Red River along the southern boundary of what is now Manitoba. Following are one or two of his references to the liquor trade.

How Notokwa, an influential old lady among the Ojibways, conducted her drinking bouts, he describes as follows: "In the course of a single day she sold 120 beaver skins, with a large quantity of buffalo robes, dressed and smoked skins and other articles, for rum. It was her habit, whenever she drank, to make drunk all the Indians about her, at least as far as her means would extend."

Frequent mention is made of his being "plagued" by the Indians for rum. Here is another note: "I gave Tabashaw, Maymiutch, and Vieux Collier each some clothing and ... a 9-gallon keg of rum. Among the others I divided three kegs of mixed liquor. ... I then, in a long speech, encouraged them to behave well, and not to be afraid of the Sioux. ... Some of their women came running into camp, bawling out that they had heard several shots fired in the meadow. I ordered the Indians to leave their liquor with me, and put off drinking till to-morrow; but they had tasted it, and must drink, at the risk of their lives."

These were Saulteaux Indians, at deadly enmity with the Sioux, who frequently invaded their territory.

Further on he relates this incident: "The Indians continued drinking. About midnight I heard one of them chopping at the gate with an ax, and bawling out ... for liquor. ... One who had received a stab in the knee during the night came over for me to dress it."

Again: "The Indians continued drinking. About ten o'clock I was informed that old Crooked Legs had killed his young wife. ... She was not dead, but had received three dreadful stabs. I went to see her; she was stretched at full length in Crow's tent, with her relations about her, bawling and crying; they were all blind drunk."

Elsewhere Henry mentions that of twenty-eight packages of goods received on one occasion for the Saulteaux trade on Red River, ten were nine-gallon kegs of "high wine."

Here and there in his narrative Henry soliloquizes at some length upon and condemns the liquor traffic, but there is no evidence to show that he did anything to stop it. This is hardly surprising. There were at this time three principal companies—the North-West, the XY and the Hudson's Bay—competing for the Indian trade in the Canadian West and fierce rivalry existed among them. This made concerted action impossible and without a common agreement to omit liquor from their stock-in-trade, all must continue to include it. Independent action by any one of them would have been suicidal. Such was the liquor traffic among the Indians of the North-West during the first half of the last century.

During my first years along the Saskatchewan, I knew personally several of the men who, in earlier days, had traded liquor among the Indians and heard from them many grimly amusing and sometimes ghastly tales of their experiences. I never met Shawman, the resourceful rascal mentioned in the narratives of Butler and Cowie, but an unusually intelligent and educated halfbreed freighter, now dead, whom I shall call Soldat, with a family name well known in Manitoba, was among my familiar acquaintances. He had been at one time in his youth a partner of Shawman and I shall relate briefly one or two of his exploits as he told them to me, prefacing his account with a short description of the manner in which a whiskey trade was conducted.

First, as to the liquor. This was usually alcohol, sixty-five over proof and altogether too fiery for use as a beverage in a raw state. Its potency and small bulk, however, made it convenient for transportation, a few gallons being a merely nominal load for the carts, and water everywhere plentiful. When within half a day's travel of the prospective site of the trade the merchant called a halt somewhere near a stream and proceeded to "mix his liquor." One keg of alcohol, or "high wine," would be diluted—originally—to make three of "mixed liquor." More water was added from time to time as the mixture took effect and the Indians gradually reached a stage where anything not exactly flavourless passed for a drink, until toward the close of the trade little of the exhilarating ingredient would be left but the smell. I have heard it said that occasionally some warrior, under its mellowing influence and out of the bigness of his heart, moved to pity through the dejection of a poverty-stricken brother, would hail him and squirt a little of the liquor from his own mouth into that of his friend.

A couple of gallons of liquor was always set aside for "the guard." These were men selected by the trader to protect himself and his wares in the camp during the trade—as a general thing a very necessary precaution. The guards were in honour bound to abstain until the trade was over, their portion of the liquor being turned over to them by the trader just before he left the camp.

Having completed his preliminary arrangements, the trader journeyed on, sending a messenger ahead to apprise the Indians of his coming. They then donned war paint and feathers and rode out in a body to meet and escort him into camp. Here he would find a lodge set up for his special use and probably a present of horses and robes, for which he was expected to make a suitable return in gifts.

There was finesse, too, in the method of dealing out the liquor, an art in which the legend of Shawman's preeminence has survived the man himself. A prime buffalo robe was worth two cups of liquor. Shawman would seize a proffered robe, scoop up a pot of liquor quickly, dash it into the Indian's pail or kettle and repeat the process. The cup, of course, was often not more than half full. If there was a complaint, Shawman handed the disgruntled customer a drink and went on with the next trade.

In the fall of 1864, my halfbreed friend was trading with Shawman among the Stoneys (Assiniboines) at Wood Mountain. An old Stoney sat on the floor of their tent, begging for liquor. At length Shawman lost his temper. A kettle with a quart of liquor in the bottom stood near him. He reached down, caught up the kettle and seizing the Indian by the neck, poured the liquor down his throat. The suppliant sputtered and gasped but he couldn't absorb it all. So Shawman turned the kettle upside down over his head. The ancient warrior struggled to his feet and reeled off, happy and singing, shouting that Shawman was "a great chief," with the liquor streaming down his back.

A little later a drunken warrior approached the tent, loudly lauding Shawman's virtues, coupled with a request that he be given some tobacco. The tobacco for the trade usually came in serons—large packages in the form of spools upon which the tobacco, three-fourths of an inch thick, was wound like rope. Shawman cut off a yard and threw it to the Indian, who then went away.

But they were not to be so easily rid of him. In a few minutes they saw him in the distance again headed for the tent, declaiming in a maudlin harangue that Shawman was a mighty chief and would no doubt give him more tobacco. He got another yard.

Now, the traders thought, their importunate publicity agent would be satisfied. They were mistaken. Less than half an hour passed when they again heard his voice and recognized that under the smoke screen of flattery he was embarked on another joyous assault on the coveted and solacing weed.

Shawman went to the roll and cut off another piece—a fathom this time, double the length of the yard. He doubled the tobacco in his hand and waited.

The Indian came on, chanting his paean of praise—*Shawman ano, chaundee waspaymiko!"* ("Shawman great chief, give me tobacco!"). As he appeared in the door, with a drunken grin on his face, Shawman's left arm shot out suddenly and he had his hand firmly fixed in the roached knot of hair above the Indian's forehead. Simultaneously, his right arm described a circle in the air and the whistling double rope of tobacco fell with a resounding crack across the bare back of the startled savage. Again the lash descended, coiling about the naked body like a snake, while the red man danced and writhed and his agonized yells brought the whole camp tumbling out of the lodges. At last Shawman dropped his arm.

The Stoney fell back a step; then drawing his knife, howling like a fiend, he came at Shawman.

He did not get far. The four guards employed by the traders stepped in and stopped him.

If Shawman's courage had been commensurate with his bulk and strength ("an ox on two legs," Soldat described him), he would have been a brave man indeed. But it wasn't. Soldat, who sat at the back of the tent, smoking and looking on, could see that the arrest was an immense relief to Shawman. However, the whole thing had lasted but a moment and now the big man bent quickly and whispered in French to his partner:

"Catch hold of me, boy!"

Soldat gaped; he did not comprehend. Shawman repeated his request, more peremptorily, and Soldat—also a big man—jumped and threw his arms about him.

Then Shawman flew into a mighty rage. He snarled, roared like a bull, gnashed his teeth, made vicious passes in the air with his own knife, while he plunged and fought in well-simulated attempts to break away from his partner and reach the Stoney.

This amazing performance on the part of the great man had a sobering effect on his antagonist. His own wrath quickly subsided as he gazed round-eyed at this towering fury and his quickly-assembled friends had no difficulty in hustling him out of harm's way and back to his lodge. Meanwhile the guards had been endeavoring earnestly to pacify the potentially-devastating trader and eventually succeeded. Peace having been restored in the tent, Shawman turned to his partner and said:

"Why didn't you catch hold of me at once, when the Stoney drew his knife. They might have thought I wasn't dangerous."

The partners had arrived in the camp with an original stock of ten gallons of alcohol which they diluted to make forty gallons of trade liquor. They left on the morning of the third day with 250 prime buffalo robes, worth at that time $7.50 each in Winnipeg, quantities of fresh buffalo tongues, dried meat and pemmican and my narrator could not recall how many horses.

Shortly after the Minnesota Massacre of 1862, when the Sioux, flying before United States troops, crossed over into Manitoba, Soldat and his brother made a trip into the southwestern part of the province to trade liquor to the refugees. Beside a creek they came upon the camps of two different clans, Wahpetons and Sissetons, a short distance apart, and began to trade.

There was no friendliness between the clans. The Wahpetons had wished to keep out of the trouble and remain in their country along the Mississippi River, but some of their young men had been drawn into it by the Sissetons, with the result that both tribes had been driven out of the state. The Wahpetons were deeply resentful and blamed the Sissetons.

The trade had not proceeded far before, the liquor taking effect, bad blood began to show itself. A drunken Sisseton approached a Wahpeton, a small but very brave man who sat smoking on the grass near the traders' tent, and began to taunt him, making light of his warlike reputation and offering to fight him. The little man at first paid no attention to his persecutor, but at length, no longer able to endure his gibes, he sprang up, swung his war hatchet and struck the Sisseton a stunning blow alongside the head with the flat of the blade. The big warrior fell like an ox.

A little later a party of Sissetons entered the soldiers' lodge of the Wahpetons with guns concealed beneath their robes. Suddenly one of them pulled his gun and shot a Wahpeton dead. More shots quickly followed.

Soldat and his brother, thoroughly scared, lost no time in putting their horses into the carts and quitting the locality. They camped some miles away.

That night the Wahpeton chief with some of his warriors visited them. Four men, he said, had been killed and as the liquor brought by the traders was responsible, they must as a penalty return to the Sioux camp and dig the graves for the dead braves. This they were forced to do, much against their wishes.

Soldat did not appear to think he had done anything requiring an apology or for which he should feel particularly ashamed. His stories were only incidents connected with the whiskey trade with the Indians, the life of the "free" traders of that day.

During the past century at least, it was never the policy of the Hudson's Bay Company to trade liquor to the Indians, except where competition made it necessary in order to procure "provisions"—dried meat, pemmican and grease—for the forts and the boat brigades which annually made the trip from the upper Peace, Athabasca, Saskatchewan, and Mackenzie rivers with the fur returns to York Factory on Hudson Bay and back with supplies for the posts for the ensuing year. At Edmonton, Pitt, Carlton and la Corne the Plains Indians could purchase liquor; farther north it was not obtainable. These Saskatchewan posts were real forts, surrounded by stout log stockades, with bastions and big guns at each corner. All gates were barred and locked and no Indian was allowed inside the fort during a rum trade. The customer passed his pemmican, meat and robes through a shutter in the stockade wall to the trader in the small house built for the purpose inside and received his portion of rum through the same opening. There might be war and sudden death outside but within the fort behind the stockade was security.

As has been said, all this is past. Even while there was still competition—in the 1850s and 1860s—the legitimate traders abolished the trade in rum. And with the arrival of the North-West Mounted Police in the early 1870s, the traffic even among the bootlegging fraternity was virtually stamped out. It was no longer profitable, when confiscation and the guardroom were the penalties exacted, to supply liquor to an Indian.

New Year's Day at a Hudson's Bay Post

It was New Year's morning at daybreak when the Doctor and myself were roused out of dreamless sleep by a round of thundering reports. It seemed as though the frost was touching off one of its mines beneath the house. We had, the day before, had a cold, forty-mile drive and felt deliciously lazy and comfortable, with an almost overpowering desire to lie late abed. Yet bed with such a racket was out of the question, so, hurrying on some essential part of our wardrobe and snatching up our guns, we rushed to the front door.

Here we came upon Uncle Joe and the source of our demoralization. He and his son were emptying their breech-loaders into the air as quickly as the attendant interpreter could remove the exploded shells and replace them with full ones. Of course we joined in the fun and helped to swell the din, which continued until the barrels grew so hot that we could hardly hold them. It was the signal to the Indians that the "master" at the fort was ready to receive them, as Hudson's Bay Company officers had, for two hundred New Year mornings before this one, made it their custom to do in each of the isolated posts of the company scattered over all British North America.

Uncle Joe was simply one of those blessed, whole-souled old boys who put so much into all that they do that ordinary terms fail entirely to convey an adequate idea of the energy with which they do it. Thus, when the salute had ended and he caught our hands in a grip that made us wince, as he wished us the happiness of the day, his face expanding into a broad grin.

"And now, my boys," said he, at length releasing our crying

Reprinted from Outing Magazine, *New York, The Holiday Number,* January 1899.

fingers, "let's get back into the house. Mrs. Mac will have finished overlooking the breakfast and we'll be none of us the worse for a bite. The air is nipping and favours strong appetites. And we'll have to dispose of the greetings first."

Answering reports began to reach us through the skirt of bare, snow-footed poplars before the post as we went inside. When we had made ourselves something more presentable and came again into the hall, Miss Maggie, a vision of loveliness in a gallant costume, a veritable fascinating Queen of Scots, with here and there a dash of bright colour, stood at the foot of the stair, and with her the principal ceremony of the day in the North began.

It was very simple and one into which the Doctor and myself entered with spirit and celerity. Miss Maggie was unquestionably a pretty girl. Later, we kissed Mrs. Mac and her younger daughters, the halfbreed domestic, and all the Indian women in the settlement, but, without meaning disrespect to anybody, I think it may be safely stated that neither the Doctor nor myself would have murmured had each of the names upon our kissing list that day been Miss Maggie.

We had barely disposed of the broiled venison and partridges and returned to the hall when the Indians, headed by their chief, came into view on the trail through the poplars. Lining up before the fort, they fired a round salute. Many of them had their faces painted.

Chief Atimoosis (Little Dog), when later he was robed in his vestments of state and abundant dignity, was a character. He had by that time put on a long scarlet cloth coat resplendent with gold lace and brass buttons, trousers of blue broadcloth with wide yellow stripes down the side, a big white felt hat with a gilt band topped by two jet-tipped eagle plumes, and beaded moccasins. Upon his ample breast rested the great silver medal given him in token of the compact made at "The Treaty" with the Great Mother, with a picture of the Great Mother, Queen Victoria, on the one side, and on the other one of his own race in a hand-clasp of friendship with a man who, like himself, wore a red coat and who was the representative of the law of the Great Mother in the land. Chief Little Dog's long, plaited hair, where it had once been all a raven black, was streaked with white, for many snows had fallen upon it. His eyes, which in his younger days had been keen and bright, were dimmed by time and his face was seared and wrinkled.

"How! How! Wachee! Wachee! (What cheer! What cheer!)" he exclaimed pleasantly, as he passed through the hall, shaking hands with Uncle Joe and the other men and solemnly kissing the ladies. When he came to Miss Maggie, either the Doctor or myself would have been glad to relieve the old man of his engagement, but he seemed nowise loath to finish it for himself. And who had a better title to kiss Miss Maggie than the aged chief? He had called upon Uncle Joe on every New Year since she was a wee chit and had religiously kissed the young lady each time as she grew step by step to womanhood with the years that passed.

The dining table was piled high with cake, pie, cold meats and bread, and large kettles of tea steamed upon the damper of the stove. Chief Atimoosis began the day, which is one of continued feasting with the Indians, by hiding away under his brass buttons liberal helpings of almost everything provided. After him came the others of the band—the minor chiefs, the bucks, and the squaws and children. They passed in at the front door and out at the back. For four hours the procession kept up, and many of the guests who had assembled from various parts of the country spent the day with hospitable Uncle Joe and his family. The Doctor and I probably did more kissing than we had done during a whole decade before.

There were old Indian women with faces which resembled nothing so much as smoked parchment, but we had to close our eyes and go through the form or be forever regarded by the "Four Hundred" of Shell River settlement with haughty disdain, as ignorant of the first law of etiquette and politeness. All were decked in holiday attire. They wore no caps, but simply shawls which were drawn about their heads like hoods. Some had fine tartan dresses and others were clothed in velvet and like expensive goods, mostly of bright colours, as blue, maroon, purple, pink, lilac and orange, but with a predominance of red.

Some of the girls were really pretty, with their olive, oval faces and handsome black hair and eyes. They wore soft mooseskin moccasins of a rich, golden smoke tan, beautifully embroidered with silk of many shades in gay floral designs, broad sashes of brave ribbon about their waists, and narrower bows of the same composing their plaited, shining tresses.

By the time dinner was announced, all the Indians had paid their respects at the fort. From here they would go to visit one another, the missionaries, the school teacher, and at each place they would drink tea and eat cake and pie, moose tongue, beaver tail, bear steak and other delicacies.

After dinner Uncle Joe had the interpreter harness his horses, and he and I started to pay the return calls upon the Indians, as befitted good manners. At the chief's were two fiddles at work and a brisk dance was in movement. The Indians of this band, as a

matter of fact, were halfbreeds who had learned something of the white man's arts, including a facility for drawing the bow over the catgut and tripping to its lively measures. I think Uncle Joe must have forgotten that he had already seen the women in the morning, for he kissed all the pretty ones over again, while everybody looked on and laughed.

Upon our homeward road we lit on a covey of white ptarmigan in a bunch of willows along the trail and succeeded in bringing down a half dozen with our guns. These beautiful birds, which are not unlike a pigeon, though larger, are usually to be found only in the extreme north and seldom come so far south as the Saskatchewan River, except in the severest winters and then only during the most snapping cold. During the summer they frequent the Barren Grounds of the north with the caribou, or reindeer, and the musk ox, and are then said to be brown in colour.

After our arrival at the house, I understood why the Doctor had pleaded laziness as an excuse for not accompanying Uncle Joe and myself on our outing. He and Miss Maggie appeared to have been improving their acquaintance of the morning and were now very good friends indeed.

During the morning a halfbreed trader, accompanied by a Chipewyan Indian, had arrived at the fort from Isle à la Crosse with two dog trains. His cap was a whole foxskin, looped round like a cuff, with the top open and the bushy tail hanging down his back. In place of a coat he wore a beaded and fringed buckskin shirt, caught at the waist with a *L'Assomption* belt, leggins of blue stroud, and moccasins. The Chipewyan was as great a stranger to the Shell River Indians as were the Doctor and I, the languages of the two tribes being entirely different, and he was certainly much more shy than either of us. The trader had a violin and could play it as well, so that we were all provided with the requirements to make of the inevitable dance to follow at the fort in the evening a memorable success.

The train dogs greatly engaged the attention of the guests. They were huge, sneaking creatures of the Husky or Esquimaux breed, with small, pointed ears and eyes and a general wolfish appearance. They snarled and fought savagely over the delicate whitefish thrown to them as food—such whitefish as one might wish in vain to have served up to one at Delmonico's—fresh, firm and fat, from the cold, untainted waters of northland lakes. They were pitched frozen to the dogs, torn apart by them with their teeth as they held the fish under their fore paws, and devoured ravenously. The stronger dogs finished their meal first and were only prevented from robbing their weaker brothers by the lash of the Chipewyan Indian.

As dusk drew on, preparations were under way for the great event of the day, or rather the night—the annual feast and dance at the fort. By six o'clock the guests began to arrive, the young halfbreed and Indian women in their finest dresses and the young men in black, with fancy silk handkerchiefs about their throats and *L'Assomption* belts. These so-called French belts are really scarfs, wrought of the finest wool in mixed bright colours and are truly very pretty. They cost the Indians at least five dollars each and are the envy of all those who have not the means to purchase them, for the French belt is the *ne plus ultra* of fashionable Indian dress; there are imitations, but they "do not count."

At seven o'clock we all filed into the long dining room, the table of which was fairly freighted with a burden of good things to eat and drink. There were two great roasts of moose meat, baked young beaver and salted wild goose, broiled hare, partridges and ptarmigan, boiled beaver tail, caribou tongues, cold moose muffle, mashed potatoes, vegetables, plum puddings, mince pies, cranberry and strawberry tarts, black tea, coffee, chocolate, raspberry vinegar and lime juice, with reindeer berry pemmican asking homage of everyone as the chief and rare titbit upon the board.

And what a feast was there, when Uncle Joe had said grace and looked down the long table with one of the broadest of his comprehensive, all-embracing grins, and the knives began to flash and the forks to play! And the chat and the laughter, in a strange babel of tongues—French, English, Cree and Saulteaux! It was bewildering altogether, and it was amazing a half hour later to look upon the wreck that had been made of that wondrous spread of eatables.

And then came the ball. Clear the hall, fling wide all the doors, tuck the seats into the corners, and all who are not nimble on their pins pack themselves into the nooks and crannies out of the way, for the night and the place belong to the devotees of Terpsichore, and they have no patience for laggard feet!

The fiddles squeak and ring and cry, the wooden walls are attuned to the strains and vibrate with sound, while moccasined soles thump time on the polished boards in jig, reel and *cotillon*, whilst the French halfbreed interpreter sings out the changes in his broken English drawl. Truly, it is a dance the like of which may be seen only in the Northland and which *must* be seen to be appreciated—especially the Red River jig. Let me try to give an idea of it:

A young Indian led out a coy, darkskinned little native to the centre of the floor. The music screeched, he bowed, and still, with joined hands, they danced up the middle and back again. Then he dropped her hand and away they went jigging separately up and down the room again, opposite one another, she with her eyes watching his feet—I was going to say invisible feet for they moved so fast they could hardly be seen—wheeling and circling round one another, here and there, and scarce seeming to touch the floor, in a "one - two - three" time, like a horse at a full gallop or the click of a passenger car over steel rails. In a few moments a second pair took the place of the first, "cutting them out" with a neat courtesy. And after a time the fiddler stopped from sheer exhaustion and the delighted onlookers yelled: *"Apeeta! Apeeta! (Half! Half!)"* and the jig struck up again, as fast and furious as ever, and lasted as long as the first "half."

The dancing was something into which the Doctor and I threw ourselves with enthusiasm. In the *Reel de huit* we were among the first to take partners. This is an exceedingly informal procedure amongst the natives in the Northland. It consists in making a more or less indefinite motion with one's hand in the direction of the lady whom one has chosen for one's partner. One does not go, necessarily, near her. He does not say: "May I have the pleasure of this dance?" or anything else, nor does he write her name on a card. After a hurried consultation with her nearest neighbours, to determine that it was really she and not one of them who had been honoured, she follows him to the position he has taken up on the floor and takes her place beside him.

The Doctor was wearing slippers and as we were wheeling through the eight-hand reel in "Elbow swing as you go," he had the luck to step out of one of them. The crowd around the walls instantly broke into a howl of ecstasy but this failed at all to ruffle the genial Doctor. He kept right on around the circle and when he came to the recreant shoe smilingly stepped into it again, amid the cheers of the natives and cries of "Bravo! Bravo!" from the whites, and so preserved the harmony of the reel.

The dance was destined, however, to come incontinently to a close, for Uncle Joe just then tossed a pound of candies into the air and a moment later all the dancers were scrambling for them on the floor.

Later in the evening the Doctor and Miss Maggie bewitched the Indians by dancing "the beautiful English dance"—a schottische—while Uncle Joe (who had no *real* nephews) played the violin. I think, too, that it must have been during our visit to Shell River Post that Miss Maggie lost her heart to the Doctor, because, not many months later, she married another man.

William Bleasdell Cameron, guide and scout to the Alberta Field Force, with Horse Child, twelve-year-old son of Chief Big Bear. They were photographed together in Regina in 1885, during the trial of Big Bear.

Agnes Emma (Bleasdell) Cameron, William Bleasdell Cameron's mother, circa 1897. Cameron Papers.

William Bleasdell Cameron, right, and family: Douglas, left; Mary Maude (Atkins) Cameron; and Owen, photographed in North Vancouver in the early 1920s. Cameron Papers.

Top left: William Bleasdell Cameron, known to his contemporaries as Bleasdell Cameron, photographed at the height of his career in 1926. Cameron Papers.

Top right: Bleasdell Cameron, right, and Saturday Evening Post writer Ross Annett, photographed in early 1940. Cameron Papers.

Bleasdell Cameron standing in the doorway of his drugstore in Derwent, Alberta, in the 1930s. Cameron Papers.

The North-West Territories as they were in 1885. Courtesy University of Saskatchewan Special Collections, Morton Papers.

Bleasdell Cameron, then with the Indian Department, riding what was called an "ordinary" or "penny farthing" bicycle at a late 1890s sports day at Duck Lake, N.W.T. Courtesy University of Saskatchewan Special Collections, Morton Papers.

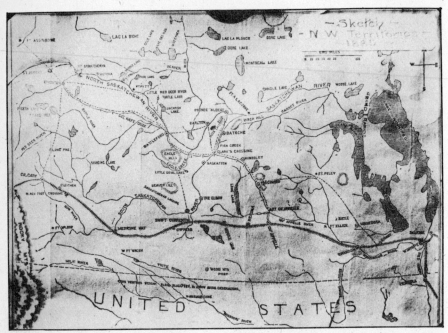

On land the Red River cart was the main burden carrier before the railway came to the northwest. Here a Metis camp is seen with four carts in evidence. *Courtesy Saskatchewan Archives Board, R-A3955.*

The river steamboat, propelled by rear paddle wheel, played an important part in early western transportation for a short period. Here the North West arrives at Battleford with General Middleton in May 1885. *Courtesy Public Archives of Canada, R-B2825.*

A husky dog team on the run. Courtesy University of Saskatchewan Special Collections, Morton Papers.

An early artist's conception of the fur canoe, the longest serving method of transportation in the early fur trade years. Courtesy Saskatchewan Archives Board, R-A8767.

The York boat followed the canoe in the fur trade. Here are two of them on Lake Winnipeg, probably photographed in the late 1800s. Courtesy Saskatchewan Archives Board, R-A4050.

A North-West Mounted Police constable with his horse, photographed circa the late 1890s. Courtesy Saskatchewan Archives Board, S-B79.

North-West Mounted Police in winter uniform at Fort Macleod in 1894. Courtesy Saskatchewan Archives Board, R-B1383.

A troop of Mounties in summer scarlet dress, probably at Regina circa 1914. Note the Indian camp in the background. Courtesy Saskatchewan Archives Board, R-B1445.

This historic photograph shows Indian chiefs and white men in the interior of Fort Pitt just before the rebellion of 1885. They are 1, Four Sky Thunder; 2, King Bird, Big Bear's son; 3, Matoose; 4, Napasis; 5, Big Bear; 6, Angus McKay, H.B.Co.; 7, Dufrain, H.B. cook; 8, L. Goulet; 9, Stanley Simpson, H.B.Co.; 10, Alex McDonald; 11, Rowley; 12, Cpl. Sletch, NWMP; 13, Edmund; 14, Henry Dufrain. Ernest Brown photo courtesy Saskatchewan Archives Board, R-B3938.

Shortly after being rescued from Big Bear's camp, Theresa Gowanlock and Theresa Delaney, both of whom lost their husbands in the 1885 massacre, sketched the scene as they remembered it. The slaughter of the white members of the community is taking place on the brow of a hill to the left. Courtesy Saskatchewan Archives Board, R-A3429.

Left: Almighty Voice. Courtesy Saskatchewan Archives Board, R-B4512.

Top right, Little Poplar in his finery; bottom right, Wandering Spirit, Big Bear's war chief, in his usual costume. Illustrations reprinted by permission of the artist, James Simpkins, were originally published in The Beaver, *September 1943, and were provided through the courtesy of the Hudson's Bay Company.*

III

THE NORTH-WEST
MOUNTED POLICE

Sir John A. Macdonald, the visionary prime minister, made a number of important moves in preparation for the opening of the huge North-West Territory that had been placed under his government's care. In 1873, legislation was passed for the establishment of the North-West Mounted Police. The following year, a body of three hundred mounted men with support staff, wagons, horses, cattle and carts, marched off in a cavalcade from Fort Dufferin (Emerson, Manitoba) toward Fort Whoop-Up where Montana whiskey traders were debasing the Blackfoot Indians. By the time they arrived, the traders had fled so the NWMP established a post on an island in the Oldman River, naming it Fort Macleod after their first Assistant Commissioner, James F. Macleod.

By the time Cameron had arrived in Winnipeg, the police had established a number of posts and detachments, linked by routes over which regular patrols were made. Their scarlet tunics were soon accepted by white and native alike as symbols of law and order fairly applied.

Peaceful Invasion

The year 1874 was marked by an epochal event in that vast expanse of territory which reached from the Red River on the east to the foothills of the Rocky Mountains on the west. The significance of that memorable year lay in the fact that it witnessed the coming to the Canadian West of a little company of intrepid spirits, recently organized in the East and named the North-West Mounted Police, bringing law, and ultimately order, to that virginal land.

The country then was virtually a wilderness. There were, it is true, a few budding settlements—handfuls of white men and women imbued with the pioneering spirit at isolated points: Fort Qu'Appelle, Prince Albert, Fort Edmonton—but by and large it was populated only by nomadic Indian tribes, eternally at war one with another, living by and on the buffalo which then pastured in herds of thousands on the lush grass that carpeted the territory from the international boundary to the Saskatchewan and Athabasca rivers.

That stout-hearted little body of redcoats were truly intrepid spirits. Almost without exception they were easterners, brought up in the provinces on the Atlantic side of the Great Lakes and with only a vague idea of the nature of the territory they were invading and its tribal inhabitants or the character of the mission on which they were embarked. That they would encounter Indians ("savages" they were called in that day) they knew, but whether they were to be received by them civilly or with unfriendliness only time would determine. They might be called upon to fight, not only these redoubtable red men, but (their immediate and primary objective) a lawless band of hard men

Reprinted from The Beaver, *Winnipeg, Man., March 1948.*

from south of the border who had established themselves behind log walls in a group of buildings they appropriately named "Fort Whoop-up," and were carrying on what, for them, was a highly profitable trade. To their customers the Indians, however, it brought only destitution and death through the whiskey they were given in exchange for their buffalo robes and wolf skins.

The first aim of the police was to put a stop to this nefarious traffic, and this they did. The conscienceless traffickers fled at the approach of the redcoats and the police found Whoop-up abandoned—abandoned, that is, except for the presence of one lone occupant.

And what had this redcoat three hundred encountered in that record breaking march? Hostility from the tribes? Suspicion? Distrust? Attack? No. The Indians received them as friends, as benefactors—as deliverers from a trade that was destroying them and from the men who were battening on it.

Now, how account for this penetration of Canada's North-West Indian Territory by complete strangers without opposition from its warlike native possessors? It was something that excited the wonder and admiration of those sections of the United States army immediately south of the border where there was a record of almost continual wars with the Indian tribes. There may be other reasons, but it is possible to point with certainty to one which may be reckoned the chief.

The North-West Mounted Police, as has been said, came west in 1874. But (and here is a significant fact) for more than two hundred years before—specifically, since 1670—the Governor and Company of Adventurers of England trading into Hudson's Bay, in other words, the Hudson's Bay Company, had been in intimate touch with the Indians. They had come, not as conquerors, but as peaceful traders, whose chief purpose was to collect as many furs as possible. They discouraged inter-tribal wars, which ruined trade, and cultivated the trust and friendship of the Indians. Aside from any altruistic considerations, this was good business. The Company was no fly-by-night, anxious to make quick profits and then retire, as were many of the independent traders and the North-West Company partners. It was in the country to stay and the Indian trapper was a vital part of its business, for without the native hunters and trappers there would have been little fur to trade. The welfare and efficiency of the Indian was thus of the utmost importance to the trader. How well the Company men succeeded in establishing friendly relations with the tribes may be judged from the words of the first lieutenant-governor of Manitoba: "The Indians of Canada have, owing to the manner in which they were dealt with for generations by the Hudson's Bay Company, an abiding confidence in the Government of the Queen."

While all this was amicably arranged, differences later arose between the whites and the Indians which threatened hostilities, and here again men of the Hudson's Bay Company stepped into the breach and helped in restoring friendly relationships. As illustration, I may here set out one of many instances in which efforts of Company officials brought about reconciliation when the passions of the red men were at fever pitch and it seemed as if nothing could avert a bloody rupture.

Indians as a race are exactly like other people—some good, others not. Kahweechetwaymot belonged in the latter category.

Kahweechetwaymot had kicked over the traces; specifically, he had offended Her Majesty the Queen, otherwise the Great White Mother, by belabouring one of her loyal servants with an axe handle. The servant was John Craig, farming instructor to the Indians of Poundmaker's Reserve. Kahweechetwaymot had gone to Craig with a request for provisions, but he hadn't got them. There followed the attack with the axe handle. And for three days Supt. L. N. F. Crozier, commanding the North-West Mounted Police at the old territorial capital of Battleford, had been on the ground at Poundmaker's striving vainly to take Kahweechetwaymot into custody and hale him to court at Battleford, where he would learn that Her Majesty was greatly displeased with her red subject and be suitably disciplined.

For two days Major Crozier had parleyed with the head chiefs—Big Bear, to whose band the culprit belonged, and Poundmaker, but the offender was still free. Moreover, he was openly boasting of attacking a white government official. As a result he was by way of being regarded by his young fellow-tribesmen as a sample of the real thing in braves. It was June of that year of 1884 and the season of the annual Thirst Dance of the Crees, so there were a lot of them on the ground; they numbered probably ten times the small force assembled to carry out the commanding officer's orders. And the chiefs had declared in no uncertain terms that if the mass of their followers would not surrender Kahweechetwaymot there was nothing they could do about it. That was how matters stood at noon of the third day, and a crisis was at hand.

Crozier had converted an old log ration house on the reserve into a makeshift fort, with a bastion at each of the two front corners and a protective slough at the rear. And now the thin line of mounted redcoats, backed by a second line on foot, was facing a mass of wildly yelling and gesticulating braves, bent on preventing the arrest of Kayweechetwaymot and ready as soon as their courage had been pumped up to the proper pitch of recklessness, to launch an attack on the police. At the moment it looked as if Canada might soon learn of a duplication on her western frontier of "Custer's last stand."

At this critical juncture a new figure appeared in the picture. He was William McKay, manager of the Hudson's Bay Company at Battleford, who had arrived on the ground that morning and had taken in the situation at a glance. He had used all his powers of persuasion to induce the chiefs to assert their authority and order the surrender of Kahweechetwaymot, but without success. They had, they told him, offered to put themselves in the custody of the police chief, but he would accept no substitute. He had come out to take Kahweechetwaymot and he meant at any cost to carry out his purpose.

Tension was mounting and McKay saw the need for immediate action. Emerging from the police line, he entered the open space separating the opposing forces and spoke sternly to the truculent tribesmen as he strode up and down before them.

"*Keeskwayawuk!* [Fools!]" he stormed, "are you mad? Do you wish to see your lodges filled with dead men and weeping women and children? You say you want to fight the police. But wait a little; if you do you are going to pay a terrible price. Suppose you wiped them out, do you think that would be the end? It would only be the beginning! The Great Mother would send her soldiers—thousands of them—and the fighting would stop only when most of you would be dead. *Payatik!* take care! Stop, before it is too late. Give this man up!"

Wandering Spirit, war chief of Big Bear's band, broke out of the Indian line and seized McKay by the wrist, attempting to drag him over to the hostile ranks. "Come!" he cried in a frenzy. "You are of our people; you cannot side with the *chemoginusuk!* You will be killed. Come over!"

McKay threw him off. Less than a year later this stormy petrel of the Crees began the massacre at Frog Lake, in which nine white men were shot to death. Wandering Spirit himself died on the scaffold the following November for his crime.

Crozier turned to Laronde, the police halfbreed interpreter: "Which is he—the man we want?"

A tall Indian, a sneer on his sinister face, danced and capered provokingly in the van of the mob. Laronde pointed. "That's him." And as the Indian, noticing, dived among his fellows, "There he goes!"

McKay called to him and the Indian came out. "Tell the police *okemow*, you'll surrender," William admonished. "You'll get a fair trial. You may be punished, but they can't hang you. Be a man; give yourself up!"

"I won't!" retorted Kahweechetwaymot.

McKay turned to Crozier. "Arrest your man," he prompted.

Crozier was scrutinizing the tumult opposite. "Think it time?"

"Yes." The defiance of the Indians had roused McKay's wrath. "The longer the delay, the greater the danger. Talk will get us no-where."

A moment's pause; then the order:

"The two men afoot on the right, fall out and nab that fellow!"

"Sligo" Kerr, his Irish up, reached Kahweechetwaymot in a bound and, with a swing that had nothing gentle about it, landed him by the plaits of his long black hair among the police. Sligo boasted later, picturesquely, if somewhat mixed-metaphorically: "The howls of the haythin were somethin' frightful to behold!"

The Indian mob broke. The hostiles swarmed about the police, stabbing at their horses with the points of their knives, hoping to stampede them; fighting to reach and release Kahweechetwaymot, stripping tunics from the backs of the redcoats. Poundmaker himself, ostensibly friendly, wrested a carbine from the grip of a constable. But the horses, like their riders, held firm until at last, wrestling and struggling, the troop reached their improvised fort and hustled their prisoner into waiting hands behind the bacon-and-flour breastworks.

Outside the fort the uproar mounted. Whoops and war cries filled the air. The Indians, furious over the successful coup of the police, were vowing vengeance.

"Looks like we'd have to fight our way out yet," Crozier remarked to McKay. The Hudson's Bay man, it appeared, didn't share the officer's dismal foreboding. "Throw out the bacon and the flour," he said.

Crozier stared. "What! Tear down our protective wall? Why—"

William nodded. "Go on, throw it out," he said again. "If I'm any prophet, you won't need the protection."

Crozier was still worried, but his confidence in McKay's judgment was limitless. The heavy sacks went over.

The effect was magical. The tumult died abruptly. The Indians had had little to eat for three days; they were hungry, ravenously hungry. They forgot their feud with the police, forgot Kahweeche-twaymot. They pounced on the provisions and in an instant were lugging them off to their lodges. And in the interval the police bundled a crestfallen brave, stripped of all belligerency, into a wagon and were on their way with him to Battleford and justice.

McKay's strategy was a winner. He knew Indians.

Laronde, left behind, was a prisoner in the hands of the hostiles. That he, one with a measure of their own blood, should have helped in the capture of Kahweechetwaymot infuriated them, and his chances of living seemed remote. McKay, who had stayed when the police left, looked him up.

"Don't be foolish," he told the halfbreed's captors. "You have no reason to blame the interpreter. He's paid to do this work. It's his job—how he makes his living." And despite fiery harangues and heated objections, McKay's eloquence in the end prevailed and Laronde was liberated.

William McKay had one more item of unfinished business to dispose of before quitting the reserve. It concerned Poundmaker.

"N'chiwam (brother)," he said, "that gun you took from the policeman, you will have to give it up."

The chief flushed angrily. "I will not!" he exploded. "He was going to use it against us."

"Now, see here," McKay spoke as if chiding an unruly child, "you mustn't look at it in that way. That gun didn't belong to the policeman; it belonged to The Great White Mother and I must take it and deliver it to the Indian agent."

Three years before, Poundmaker had guided the Marquis of Lorne, the Queen's son-in-law and then Governor-General of the Dominion, three hundred miles across the plains from Battleford to the Blackfoot Crossing, and he greatly impressed His Excellency, who made much of the stately and handsome red man. Poundmaker had not forgotten this and he did not wish to offend the noble lord's mother-in-law. So McKay secured the carbine.

Four of us—volunteer reinforcements—armed and mounted, were on our way to Poundmaker's on the third day of the trouble. The afternoon was intensely hot, and we had stopped to breathe our dripping horses and quench our thirst from the cool water of Medicine Drum Creek when we saw a rider approaching from the direction of the reserve. He gave us the high sign.

"The fun's all over, boys," he bawled. "They're coming in with the prisoner. You might as well go home."

Kahweechetwaymot had a part in the butchery at Frog Lake in the following April; but he was more fortunate than Wandering Spirit and the seven other murderers hanged with him. He escaped the noose. In the battle of Frenchman's Butte, on May 28th, a shell fragment stripped the flesh from his leg, and he died before dawn next day.

Riders of the Plains

Does the average British soldier ever know fear? He has ridden unfalteringly against broad-mouthed cannon belching red death upon him at Balaklava and other places, "for the honor of Old England." Only the other day a roughly-organized band under a gallant if hasty leader, galloped a hundred and fifty miles with a pocketful of ammunition and no food to mention, to attempt the overthrow of a republic of superb marksmen, outnumbering them twenty times, with whose politics they disagreed. And in the summer of 1874 a little company of three hundred took their lives in their hands and marched nine hundred miles across an unknown wilderness to the feet of the Rockies, put down an illicit liquor traffic carried on with its thirty thousand of a savage population, and practically added a territory as large as Europe to the British Crown without a single fight.

To be sure this was only the first step in the conquest, which has been pursuing and making good its right to the title steadily year by year ever since, until now the right is established. But the first step had to be taken; and let not the fact that the conquest has been in the main a bloodless one detract from the glory of it. That two thousand mile march over the plains and back will one time fill a greater page in history than it does today, and the North-West Mounted Police be accorded that standing among the warrior-servants of the Empire to which their deeds entitle them.

Yet the North-West Mounted Police were not organized as a military force; they were not expected to subdue the country by the power of arms, but, in the language of their motto, to

Reprinted from Toronto Saturday Night, *Toronto, Ont., May 23, 1896.*

"Maintain the right." They are the embodiment of a conception of Sir John A. Macdonald.

The three hundred men who left Dufferin, Man., (two miles north of Emerson) in July, 1874, under Col. French, formerly of the Royal Artillery, carried with them, besides their rifles and small arms, two field pieces and two mortars. Col. Macleod was assistant commissioner. The country over which they travelled was parallel to that now traversed by the Canadian Pacific Railway but much closer to the Canada/U.S. border for about 200 miles, then they turned northwest toward Cypress Hills and away from the border. But one who glides today smoothly and swiftly across our great West in a Pullman palace car, can form no idea of the obstacles which were then met and surmounted.

Alkali water, thick and milk-coloured, played frightful havoc among their horses; their commissariat was meagre (though buffalo meat, which was often to be had for the killing when they arrived on the prairie formed a welcome addition to it); and their clothing was in rags before half the distance to Macleod had been covered. Added to the discomforts was the danger of attack from the savages, whose knowledge of the white man and his ways was derived mainly from a pack of outlaws, who robbed them of their sustenance in exchange for liquid poison which caused men to slay their brethren, and who were consequently prone to take alarm and the offensive.

Rumours reached them, too, of whiskey traders in force at their rendezvous, Fort Whoop-Up, on the Belly River, near the present site of Fort Macleod, who would make a stubborn resistance. But if the outlaws had ever harboured such a thought they must have abandoned it, for the Police, upon their arrival, found Whoop-Up empty as the surrounding desert save for one trader, a few Indians, but no liquor.

Col. Macleod, who succeeded to the commissionership in 1876, built the old fort which was named for him. His first care was to place himself upon a friendly footing with Crowfoot, the head chief of the allied Blackfoot tribes, and so well did his efforts in this direction prosper that when Sitting Bull, with his hostiles, crossed the border after the Custer battle of 1876, Crowfoot resisted all the overtures made to him by the Sioux chief to join him in a war of extermination against the whites. Later, Major Walsh made a fast friend of Sitting Bull; the Sioux kept the peace during their five years' stay upon Canadian soil, and if we do not owe it entirely to Major Walsh and his command, their masterly handling of the aliens compelled a confidence and respect which assuredly was not without its influence in preventing trouble on more than one occasion.

In 1880 Colonel Macleod was appointed to the bench, and Colonel Irvine was made Commissioner of the Force. In the following year the Police accomplished that marvelous march of over two thousand miles at an average of thirty-five miles a day, on Lord Lorne's escort, which called forth the outspoken admiration, not only of the Governor-General and his staff, but also of the London press and the chiefs of the Imperial army.

The original plan had been to divide the force between Fort Edmonton and Swan River. They both became police strong points but other points to the south such as Fort Walsh, Fort Calgary, Fort Macleod, Fort Saskatchewan, Fort Carlton, became police strong points as well. By 1881 sixteen major posts were in operation and in 1882 the Force was increased to five hundred men.

In 1883, the Force received unstinted and merited praise for the excellent order preserved during the building of the Canadian Pacific Railway through the territory of the Blackfoot, who were disturbed by the advance of the white men in such numbers, and of the "iron horse," and feared they were to be driven from their heritage.

After the Riel Rebellion of 1885, when the commissioner, Col. Lawrence Herchmer, succeeded to that position, the Police were increased again, to one thousand. At the present time [1896] the strength is about eight hundred, in eight divisions of (nominally) one hundred each.

Following is a list showing the number of officers in the Force, with their respective salaries. There are about one hundred and sixty non-commissioned officers, and nearly six hundred constables, scouts and supernumeraries. The pay of constables ranges from fifty to seventy-five cents a day, and of non-commissioned officers from seventy-five cents to a dollar and a half.

1896 Officers' Pay

Commissioner	$2,400
Assistant Commissioner	1,600
Eight Superintendents	1,400
Twenty-nine Inspectors	1,000
Five Assistant Surgeons	1,000
Two Veterinary Surgeons	1,000

Commissioned officers are upon the regular superannuation list. Under the present Police Act, provision is made for pensions for the enlisted men after ten years' service, and the term of enlistment is five years. Originally the term was but three, and though no pensions were allowed, a constable's pay was a dollar a day for the whole of his term and he received a land grant of one hundred and sixty acres ($160 land scrip) at the close of it.

Perhaps the most important work falling to the Force today is patrols, and a map of the country showing the police trails looks like a spider's web. Along the International boundary alone is seven hundred miles, all of which is covered regularly every few days by our "Riders of the Plains" in red. They guard Her Majesty's customs, head off drifting Yankee cattle, observe the peculiar matrimonial proclivities of the Mormons with a view to possible disruptures of their domestic felicities, catch horse and other thieves and murderers, sleep under the stars, ride frequently fifty to one hundred miles a day, and do several other strange and amusing things.

Excellent good feeling prevails between them and their cousins in arms and blue over the border, and they are always ready to act together for the circumvention of crime. In 1895 a detachment of twenty, under Inspector Constantine, was sent into the Yukon to look after the customs and preserve order in that region, and detachments are also stationed at Athabasca and other points in the farther North where the territory is still under prohibitory liquor law.

Various means of recreation and amusement are provided at the larger posts. At Regina, the headquarters of the Force, there are reading and billiard rooms, a gymnasium and entertainment hall; and at all divisional headquarters there are now canteens and reading rooms. At Regina they also have a piano, and in fact wherever half a dozen policemen are found together, the "Heavenly Maid" is seldom an entire stranger. Everywhere are amateur musicians—the trill of the flute, the tinkle of the banjo, the ring of the violin. The regimental bands at Regina and Calgary are perhaps the best in the North-West; and a prettier sight it would be hard to imagine than the Depot Division Mounted Band on a warm summer afternoon on parade, the sun glancing from the burnished instruments and lighting up the scarlet and gold of the bandsmen's uniforms, while in perfect order the horses with arched necks step proudly to the time of the music. An officer always accompanies the band; the Depot Division Band was the especial pride of late Inspector "Tommy" Wattam, its adjutant, and one of its best officers.

In summer, cricket, football, shooting, boating, riding and other out-of-door sports prevent the time from dragging upon the Policeman who happens not to be upon active duty; while in winter snowshoeing and skating, driving, gymnastics, hunting, minstrel shows, dancing and reading make the time pass very pleasantly.

(Since this was written the NWMP became "Royal" NWMP (1904). The force became responsible for all of Canada west of Thunder Bay (1918). It was named Royal Canadian Mounted Police (1920) and continued to grow in strength and responsibility. Already enforcing federal laws it undertook to enforce provincial statutes: in Saskatchewan (1928); Manitoba, Alberta, New Brunswick, Nova Scotia and Prince Edward Island, (1932); British Columbia and Newfoundland, (1950). A marine division was formed (1932) as was an air division (1935). RCMP contracts to enforce municipal laws in about two hundred municipalities. The Force served in both World Wars. Its strength today (1985) is approximately 20,000, headed by a Commissioner with rank of deputy minister reporting to the Solicitor General of Canada—Editor)

Sergeant Kay's Capture
(Fiction)

First post had gone on the bugle at Fort Saskatchewan, and the major was sitting on the porch of his quarters, discussing with his adjutant the details of a practice march arranged the following week for B Troop. The hard blue of the sky changed to purple, then to steel gray, and Saturn appeared low down on the western horizon. Over the level stretches of the prairie the night wind blew softly, rustling the yellow grass. It was peculiarly soothing to the two officers, smoking in lazy contentment after an arduous day in the blazing August sun.

They paused in their chat, and their thoughts drifted to other lands; they saw faces, the pensive faces of women and the laughing ones of little children, while they watched the stars come out, one by one, in the deepening dusk. They remembered that those same stars shone over the homes which sheltered those women and children; they seemed like sentinel eyes keeping tireless vigil over those loved ones, separated from them by long leagues of hill and plain and by the vicissitudes of a soldier's calling; and their hearts warmed to their friendly twinkling.

At length the major's vagrant thoughts reverted to the matter in hand. "Thirty miles will do for the first day," he resumed. "That will take you into the Beaver Hills, where there's good camping; now the cool nights keep the flies down. How's regimental number 2142?"

"All right again, sir," said the adjutant. "Slight attack of influenza, the veterinary surgeon said it was. He'll——"

The door of the guard house across the square opposite swung open and a bugle rang out shrilly on the quiet night air. The two

Reprinted from The Argonaut, *San Francisco, Calif., March 20, 1899. This story is likely based on fact.*

officers sprang to their feet. A shot went off, followed by another and another. Forms flitted back and forth through the bars of light which streamed across the parade ground from the barrack windows. The officer of the day hurried up, touched his hat, and said:

"I have to report, sir, that the prisoners McCorkle and Milligan have overpowered the guard and escaped."

The major muttered something not on record, took three strides up the porch and two back, and then rapidly delivered his orders:

"Detail Kay and Hatherton to scout south toward Blindman's River; they'll probably work round to that vicinity, sooner or later. Send Smith and Edmonds north to the Athabasca Landing, and Murphy and Kraus east as far as Saddle Lake. Fontaine and Christianson can take the north bank of the Saskatchewan as far as Lac Ste. Anne."

Twenty minutes later the four details pulled out of Fort Saskatchewan on a blind search for as choice a pair of blacklegs as might have been found anywhere within a hundred miles.

Up to the winter before, some of the Fort Saskatchewan fellows had cultivated the idea that they knew a little about the game of poker, but after "Crackerbox"—baptized William McCorkle—had dwelt among them for a month they had been driven stubbornly to the conviction that somehow they had made an error of judgment. A little earlier, Calgary had been a flower, a night-blooming cereus, from the professional gambler's point of view, but the bloom had worn off; it had become too slow and staid, and Crackerbox had heard of the Saskatchewan game and moved north. He thought there might be a profitable opening for him there, and he was correct.

His operations at the green table had been quite satisfactory to himself and necessarily anything but satisfactory to anyone else. Still, the game went on, and Crackerbox continued to pull down his jackpots with complacent regularity, until one night things happened. It had been his deal, of course. He was discovered with four nines in his hand, and as three were held among the other players round the board, Crackerbox was called on for explanations, which he gave—at the point of a six shooter.

They carried the wounded man home and Crackerbox to the guard house. He had done fatigue duty on the woodpile and round the kitchen sink under the eye of an unsympathetic sentry and, while he did not say so, thought it was no sort of occupation for a gentlemanly professional gambler. He had been awaiting with feelings of deep distrust the departure of the next stage, which should carry him to the territorial pen to abide events while the sick man lingered. Perhaps they would even show so little deference to his sensitiveness there as to put him on the stone pile with absconding bank officers and other low violators of the law! The thought made his nostrils curl. "But now," as he said to himself on the night of his escape, "we have changed all that." The stage would depart without him.

Milligan, the other fugitive, was a promoter; and Milligan was in trouble, as promoters now and then are apt to be. He had been the chief instrument in the mutiny that had occurred in B Troop three months before and was serving a year at hard labour in the guard house for his zeal in a cause which had been promptly frowned down.

Early in the morning on the third day after the escape, two cavalrymen were riding across the prairie toward a distant log shack beside the trail which connected Calgary with Fort Saskatchewan. It was a stopping place for travellers and the only house in twenty miles.

"They'll sure stop at Bennet's and eat," said Sergeant Kay. "We'd best not ride too close." They drew aside into a bluff of poplars and fastened their horses among the trees. "Now," continued the sergeant, "take a walk to the right and come in below the window in the back of the shack. That knoll and the stacks will give you all the cover you require; mind, you don't show yourself. I'll shy round by the left and get to the front door. When it opens, hold your gun on 'em from the window."

Inside Bennet's, two men were breakfasting at a rough pine table. From the manner in which they ate, it might have been inferred that it was long since they had tasted food.

"Hell!" said the smaller of the two, a youngish, compact, sallow man, with a carefully pointed, narrow black moustache, pausing for a minute as Bennet set a second heaping plate of meat on the table. "This is great! It would take all B Troop to chase me from such a feed."

"Elegant," assented his companion, with a mouth full of steak. "Shtill, I'm not askin' to see any av th' clan. Ut's good riddance, any ways ye take ut, an' I hope ther's as many moiles betune us as ther' is behoind us."

The door creaked a trifle on its wooden hinges. Crackerbox looked round quickly. Sergeant Kay stood in the doorway with a levelled revolver in his hand.

"I'll trouble you, McCorkle," he said, easily. "*Oaka*—quick now! You know the formula."

The gambler's hands went up. Milligan raised his at the same instant. His eyes were engaged at the window before him.

"'Bout face!" Milligan came round mechanically, in obedience to the sharp word of command. "Tut! tut!" Kay went on protestingly; "you needn't strike your dukes, Milligan. Keep 'em up, keep 'em up. They look first rate as they are. Hatherton, walk round here—I'll do the honors while you're coming, and fit these new cuffs on the gentlemen. I want to see how they look. Cutest thing in the market; lots of starch in 'em and polished to make a Chinese laundry ashamed of itself. We haven't had a chance to try 'em on a real eligible candidate before."

He bowed with mock deference to the gambler. Crackerbox smiled amiably in return.

"I'm right glad to see you, sergeant," he said. "Seems just like home again. Funny how things turn out, ain't it? I was just wonderin' if you wouldn't happen along—and here you were! Well, all's fair in love and war—and a fox chase. Some fools in my shoes would probably see things—ropes, beams, and hornpipes. I don't. Life's too short to waste in speculation over what probably wouldn't occur. Play your game out and keep on lookin' happy. That's good clean philosophy for a man. And if you do pass out before the rest of the players, why you're only a hand ahead, and they'll be hot in your moccasin tracks to the Sweet By-by. We only just hit the ranch an hour before you, and seein' we was here first we can't do less than make you welcome. You wouldn't have grudged us a hearty reception, I know, if it had happened the other way round." Crackerbox laughed. "We was right hungry. Mr. Bennet, here, was so good as to fix us up a real enjoyable meal, an' we've just wolfed it." And, as the handcuffs went on: "And them bracelets! *Ain't* they charming! Such finish! Do you know, sergeant, as soon as I'm out o' this I'm a-going to get me a pair, gold—miniature, you know—same pattern, to hang on my watch chain as a souvenir? What's wrong, Milligan? You don't look pleased."

The big Irishman glowered under his thick red eyebrows. "I suppose this is another twelvemont' for me," he growled.

Crackerbox burst into a loud laugh. "Don't be downhearted, me son," he returned. "They can't give me too much of a good thing. I'll ask them to let me have it."

"Well, Mr. McCorkle," said Kay, "now you're wearing government jewelry, we can be more sociable. I guess you haven't finished your breakfast yet. It's ahead of anything you're likely to get between this and the fort—which is ninety miles away—so you'd best make the most of it. Jump in. And since you're so hospitable, if Mr. Bennet will be good enough to fry a little more steak, we'll eat with you. I guess you know better than to make any breaks," he added, significantly, looking from one prisoner to the other.

"Too busy to think of it," returned Crackerbox, sitting down to the table again. "Kind of a tough proposition, this, sergeant," he added a moment later, after an ineffectual attempt to cut his meat; "tryin' to handle a meal with your wrists sawin' one against the other, like cattle in a yoke."

Kay glanced at Hatherton. "Help him out, won't you?" he said. "Mr. Bennet will do the same for the other man, I'm sure."

"Oh, I can't allow that!" protested the gambler. "I'll manage." He seized the meat in his fists and tore it between his teeth, like a dog.

"Here, quit that!" exclaimed Kay. "You're a human, at least—not an animal." He took out his keys and unlocked one handcuff. "There, I'll let you eat decently and not like a pagan if you'll promise not to try to escape."

A sudden brightness flashed into the gambler's eyes, but there was nothing of it left in the look he turned on Kay, as he replied, with a bland smile: "Sure thing. I'd promise anything under the circumstances. That's easy. I say, sergeant, you're real obliging. I'll see that you're mentioned in orders."

"See that you keep your promise; that'll be sufficient," said Kay, shortly, unlocking a handcuff of the other man.

Crackerbox laughed provokingly. "Now, sergeant, I like your jokes. You two loaded down with deadly weapons, and us——"

Sergeant Kay was naturally a kind man. Also, he dearly loved a game of poker and, therefore, perhaps unsuspected by himself, nurtured a secret admiration for this cool desperado who looked on life as a game of chance and took good or ill luck indifferently as it came, with imperturbable good humour. But perhaps it was hardly discreet of the sergeant to allow his amiable disposition to influence him to the extent of freeing his prisoners' hands.

During the meal the talk drifted to poker. Kay knew enough about the game to have lost most of his pay for a year before, so he was interested in Crackerbox's professional skill. And when the gambler pushed back his chair after finishing his coffee and remarked: "Just let me show you how that's done, sergeant, before you put the bracelets on again," and walked over to another table on which lay a pack of cards, Kay did not demur. He might learn something which would help him retrieve his losses, or perhaps even do better than that.

Hatherton was interested, too, and stood beside the sergeant.

Milligan was still eating. Account for it as you may, they appeared to have forgotten him—perhaps because he had once been a fellow of B Troop with a blank defaulter sheet. Bennet apparently knew all he wanted to about poker; he bustled around, banging his tin dishes and pans. The noise enabled Milligan to slip up behind the troopers unobserved.

"You see," said Crackerbox, picking up the thread of his story again, "there was fifteen hundred dollars in the pot and they'd all dropped out except Wat Batty and me. I took the deck in my left hand"—it was extremely interesting—"like this, and 'Cards?' says I. 'I want one,' says Bat. I gave it to him. 'I'm taking three, myself,' says I, while he looked at his hand, and I took 'em. They were good ones, and they came right out o' the deck *here*, like that—see?"

"Hands up!" It was Milligan who spoke. The two troopers faced about and each looked into the unfriendly muzzle of his own revolver which Milligan had deftly extracted from its holster as he leaned over its possessor's shoulder.

"Get thim up, now, quick!" he repeated.

Crackerbox laughed his exasperating laugh. "Yes, I would if I was in your place, sergeant," he remarked. "Everything has been real pleasant so far between us this morning and we wouldn't like to have any misunderstanding, now we're about parting from you. Oblige us. Did you notice how that game came out? Funny how it goes, ain't it? Luck with you one minute an' the next it's with the other feller. I didn't know you understood the sign language so well, Milligan. You tumbled handier than a tailed steer. You must have belonged to the Invincibles before you left the ould counthry. What was your number?"

Bennet looked on stoically while, with some difficulty, Crackerbox removed the handcuffs and replaced them on the wrists of his late captors. In accomplishing this the gambler hit upon what he regarded as a neat arrangement. He stood Kay and Hatherton back to back and divided a pair of the cuffs between them on either side, securely linking them together. Bennet did not propose to risk his health in any attempt to uphold the dignity of the law. Why should he? From an abstract point of view it seems rather a peculiar fact that there should so seldom be apparent any strong general antipathy toward the man who has done nothing worse than shoot another man openly. It is only the wretch who lays unrighteous hands upon a woman—the Bill Sikeses of this world—who find all doors of hope, of human forgiveness and forbearance shut against them.

"You've been real hospitable, Mr. Bennet, and I just hate to put you out any; but there are times, you understand, when a man has to burn all his crossed bridges, and this looks to me like one of the times. It's quite a ways to where we're going and I guess you won't hold it against us if we rope you up with the others."

They bound Kay's and Hatherton's ankles, and Crackerbox walked Bennet to his bunk in the corner and tied him on it, hand and foot. Then, as he stood with his back to the others, he pulled a bill out of the silk handkerchief about his neck, winked and held it up so that the host could see the "50" printed on the corner, and then pushed it into Bennet's waistcoat pocket. Milligan then went to the corral, turned out Bennet's stock, and brought the troop horses from the bluff.

"Well, so long, sergeant," said Crackerbox, as he stood beside Kay's saddle. "We'd be glad to spend another half hour in your company but you understand we've no time to waste in social entertainment. We thank you for a real pleasant mawnin' and for bringin' down these hosses for our use. My feet was plumb playin' out, but I reckon we'll get on now. If you look real hard, boys, you'll find the keys of them cuffs in the grass not more'n a hundred yards from here; and, Bennet, your hosses won't stray so far but what you'll be able to pick 'em up to-morrer. Good day, sergeant. If you ever come down my way, look me up. I won't forget your consideration. I won't, honest."

He sprang into the saddle and clattered off, but at a hundred yards he stopped and drawled over his shoulder:

"And, oh, I say, sahgeant, remembeh me to the majah! And tell him I said, with my compliments, he wa'n't to fo'get to mention you in orders!"

Then the outlaws spurred across the prairie in the direction of that Line beyond which lay another government, driving Bennet's loose horses before them, and that was the last the two troopers saw that day of Crackerbox and Milligan.

In after years I sat often of an evening over Scotch with Kay, when he no longer wore government clothes or nursed an ambition to shine at poker, but had married a girl and settled down to raising cattle and a family. He spoke of many things, but he never told me what his feelings were as he lay through that hot August afternoon on the floor at Bennet's, counting the slow hours, until a traveller came along near dusk and released him, and I never asked. There are subjects which may not be touched upon even between friends.

The Vicious Circle at Fort Pitt

A man who went scouting in territory temporarily dominated by hostile Indians, realized that he had no assurance of returning—whole, perforated or at all. Nevertheless, as far back in America as memory goes, men were always to be found ready to take that chance. And every man who took it, confident in his personal prowess or his superior canniness, believed doubtless that what had happened to others of his acquaintance, or of whom he knew, would not happen to him. Else, unless the urgency was great, he might not have taken it. Take Corporal Dave Cowan, of the North-West Mounted Police at Fort Pitt, for example.

Cowan had just been promoted from constable, and when Captain Francis J. Dickens, son of the novelist, commanding at Fort Pitt, on April 14, 1885, called for volunteers for a delicate mission, Cowan promptly stepped to the front. If he beat Constable Clarence Loasby and Special Constable Henry Quinn in stepping, it was by a margin so small that you would not have noticed it. The only thing that would have bothered the three volunteers would have been quicker stepping on the part of others, which might have robbed the corporal and his two companions of the coveted crack at this trip.

Frog Lake was thirty-five miles distant. On the second of that same month, Big Bear's band of Plains Crees, rising treacherously overnight, had practically wiped out the little settlement, beginning the diabiolical business with the murder of Tom Quinn, the American who filled the post of Indian agent for the Canadian government at that point. Henry Quinn was his nephew. Warned by a friendly Wood Cree, young Quinn had stolen out of Frog

Reprinted from The Grain Growers Guide, *Winnipeg, Man., May 1,* 1926.

Lake, unseen and afoot, twenty minutes before the massacre commenced. He had reached Pitt next day and been sworn in by Captain Dickens as a "special." White men were scarce around Pitt—Dickens had just twenty-five under him—and there were three hundred Indians, it was not known just how far away, ready, if events proved propitious and the medicine good, to make them a lot scarcer. More than ready, in fact. They had readiness to burn.

Following the massacre, a portentous silence had fallen upon the land and it was because Dickens wanted to know and didn't—whether the Indians had moved and what they were doing—that he had called for volunteers.

The trail from Fort Pitt to Frog Lake is a fairly good one in summer, but the three scouts did not follow it. They went out along the river, which runs a few miles to the south of Frog Lake. They travelled slowly, reconnoitering the ground ahead from commanding rises, and not until sunrise next morning were they looking through their glasses from the wooded slopes across the chain of lakes at the site of the Frog Lake settlement and the two hundred lodges a short way beyond.

They observed a number of things. First, that where the settlement had been there was no longer anything but a collection of charred and deserted ruins. Again, that the camp was still where Quinn had last seen it—at least the lodges. The most important thing of all they also noticed, but unfortunately its significance did not then strike them. This was the fact that very little life was observable about the camp. Why, the little scouting detail was to discover later to its cost.

When Corporal Cowan and his companions left Frog Lake on their return to Pitt—I give the story mainly as it was told to me by Quinn—they again avoided the trail. The Indian camp was behind them, true, but hostile parties might be prowling about the country and the white men had no desire to run into a band that would likely greatly outnumber them. As they drew near Fort Pitt, however, without having sighted an enemy, they put aside a caution they now considered unnecessary and struck over to the trail. Quinn always maintained this was contrary to his advice, but Cowan was in command.

They had not followed it far until they saw that the trail was marked by many hoofprints. Quinn dismounted and examined it closely.

"I'm right, Cowan!" he exclaimed at length. "I said the Indians were ahead of us and they are. They've come down the trail as we went out along the river. Here's the track of a shod horse—my uncle's mare, that Wandering Spirit took the day of the massacre. I put those shoes on myself. I know them."

Cowan disagreed. "The police have been out during the day, rounding up the stock. That accounts for the shod tracks. The whole camp was at Frog Lake still, wasn't it?"

"The camp, yes—the lodges. But remember we saw mighty few Indians."

"Well, I'm not scared, if you are," Cowan said. "We're going on. Funk, Quinn, that's what's got you."

To which Quinn retorted angrily that he could go anywhere Cowan dared. They rode on in silence, but as it happened Quinn was right and Cowan wrong.

Pitt was now little more than a mile away and just over the crest of the slope behind it, out of sight of the fort, three hundred blood-drunken and painted savages were discussing energetically plans for getting the police outside the walls of the fort so that they might shoot them down with no risk to themselves.

The camp lay just to the left of the trail. Behind it a fringe of willows marked the course of a creek, and a break in this fringe at one point showed where the trail crossed the creek over a bridge.

When the three scouts looked from the bridge through the opening and saw the hostile camp ahead and to their left, they realized that they had made a mistake in quitting the river for the trail. But it was now too late to rectify it. Putting spurs to their horses, they dashed for the top of the slope.

The Indians saw them. Grabbing their guns, with wild cries of "Chemoginusuk! Chemoginusuk! (Soldiers! Soldiers!)" they rushed for the trail to head them off.

Along its crest to the right of the trail, the slope was thickly wooded, shutting off any chance of getting through to the fort in that direction. They had no option but to stick to the trail.

It has been said that a man does not die until his time comes, and the tragedy of that wild ride through the Indian camp rests in the fact that the three men had come unscathed through the hail of lead and then, with safety just ahead, Cowan's horse, crazed no doubt by the excitement, stopped suddenly and—bucked!

In vain Cowan spurred him; he would not budge. Cowan dropped to the ground and ran. An Indian, his gun levelled on the policeman, raced alongside. Cowan put out a hand.

"Don't my brother!" he cried in Cree, and the Indian turned and left him.

But a puff of smoke came from the wood on the right, and with a bullet through his heart, poor Cowan pitched his length along the dusty trail.

Henry Quinn's escape down the hill by way of the trail had been cut off, and answering the fusilade of which he was the target with repeated shots from his own rifle—fortunately for himself later without doing any damage—he swung at top speed to the right along the wooded slope and disappeared among the poplar bluffs up the river. The hostiles were too intent upon the capture of Fort Pitt to go after him.

Meanwhile Loasby was pounding down the slope in full view of the fort and safety as fast as his jaded mount would bear him. Lone Man—cool, crafty, daring, a human hawk, whose clear brain never permitted his nerve or confidence to desert him—with flapping pinion of soiled white blanket, on the white racer that had unaccountably disappeared from his owner's stable one dark night a year before in Montana, followed swiftly after him.

A shot. The saddle under Loasby seemed suddenly to have grown hot. Blood trickled down his leg, but he rode on. Another shot. His horse stopped, swayed, a bullet in his neck.

Lone Man was close behind—too close. The chest of the white racer hit like a hammer on the rump of the policeman's stricken mount and down they went, over and over, the dying animal and the living, falcon redskin and wounded trooper.

Loasby was first on his feet. Other Indian riders, he could hear, were racing toward him. He did not stop to look round but ran.

Lone Man raised on one knee, and at the crack of his rifle Loasby tumbled with his face in the dust and the trail of a bullet through his body close to the spine.

And now the burst of fire which, since Loasby was apparently past the possibility of injury from it, there was no longer need to hold, came upon the intrepid savage from the fort. But Lone Man writhed forward, on his belly like a snake, till he reached the policeman. He turned him over.

"I thought he was dead," Lone Man told me later, "or I would have finished him. But he ought have killed me. He came round first."

Drawing his knife, the Indian cut the belt, with its cartridges and revolver, circling Loasby's waist. Then he writhed back with it, gripping the grass with his crimsoned fingers, to his horse, and galloped away up the slope. And all the while the bullets from the fort plugged viciously into the sod around him.

There was good stuff in Loasby. He got on his feet again. He staggered to the gate of the fort, flung out derisive fingers in the direction of Lone Man and collapsed in the arms of the two troopers sent out to meet him.

Henry Quinn halted in a grove of poplars a mile up the river from the fort, dismounted and tied his horse to a tree. Night fell, and under cover of the river bank he crept cautiously down to the road leading from the fort to the stream. He could not approach the stockade in the darkness; the sentries would take no chances. Or a prowling Indian might pick him off.

He drew his knife and dug for hours in the clay bank for shelter. A blinding blizzard had come up, it lashed him like a thousand whips. The cold gripped him; he shook violently. He must have protection from the storm. At length he had a hole, big enough to shield his body from the swirling smother. He crawled in. He was ravenous. If only he had something—a crust, even!

The night dragged. At dawn he stood outside the stockade, calling for Sergeant Martin. An upper window in one of the fort buildings opened. It framed the curling black head of Wandering Spirit. Fort Pitt was in the hands of the Indians!

Again there was a cry of "*Chemoginusuk!*" and a moment later Wandering Spirit was following a fresh footprint through the newly-fallen snow. It led to the river; there ending abruptly. The war chief stood on the bank, studying the mystery of the vanishing track. Where could he have gone, this policeman? The riddle was unsolvable, and presently he walked on along the bank, rifle in hand, searching every angle of the surroundings with his hawk-like eyes.

Another Indian, Isadore Mondion, the same who had warned Quinn at Frog Lake, followed the footprints from the fort to the river and stopped. Just beneath him a pair of legs stuck out of the bank. With one hand he motioned to the war chief, with the other he pointed downward. Wandering Spirit started toward him, running.

"Henry," said Mondion, "come out."

The poor scout, hiding like an ostrich, trembled but he did not move.

"Come out, quick!" Mondion repeated sternly. "Before Wandering Spirit comes. I will protect you."

Quinn crawled from his hole. The war chief, his rifle held threateningly before him, hurried up. Mondion put a hand on Quinn, stepping in front of him.

"My prisoner, *Kahpaypamahchakwayo!*" He met the war chief's lowering glance with one no less truculent. "Be careful! His life is mine and I give it to him. From today we are brothers, him and me."

Wandering Spirit's answer, Quinn thought, would never come. But at length, with a wave of his hand, "So be it, *Neestas*," he agreed. "But the life you give him, if he loves it he will know better than to work against us. He was with the police. And his rifle—that must be mine."

The rifle was surrendered, and Mondion, his arm about his adopted brother, walked with him into the fort.

The warriors crowded round Quinn. "His medicine is very powerful!" they cried. "*Mistahay muskowow!* Bullets will not pierce him! Three times he has escaped!"

"How! How!" shouted the camp. And Quinn was safe.

IV

THE FROG LAKE MASSACRE

With the influx of white settlement, many Metis families from Red River pulled up their roots and travelled further west to Batoche-St. Laurent country on the South Saskatchewan River. There, however, they still felt threatened by the government's system of surveying, and the slowness with which titles were produced for the land they had already cleared, seeded and built upon. The Metis spoke of open revolt and sent to Montana for Louis Riel, their leader during the Red River uprising.

Meanwhile, the Indians had suffered the loss of their buffalo herds and were experiencing hardship and starvation on their reserves. One of the last holdouts was Plains Cree chief Big Bear who, in the autumn of 1884, had taken his people to the Fort Pitt-Frog Lake area. There, in March 1885, the shocking news swept the area that the Metis had defeated the Mounted Police and Prince Albert Volunteers in a conflict at Duck Lake. Would the Indians rise now? On April 2, 1885, they did; it went down in history as the Frog Lake Massacre.

The Massacre

The congregation was kneeling.

A moment later Wandering Spirit entered. He wore his lynx skin war bonnet, with its five big eagle plumes, and carried a Winchester across his arm. He dropped on one knee in the centre of the church, resting the butt of his rifle on the floor. His eyes burned and his hideously painted face was set in lines of ferocious intensity. Never shall I forget the feelings his appearance excited in me, as he half-knelt, glaring up at the altar and the white-robed priests in sacrilegious mockery. He was a demon, a wild beast, roused, ruthless, thirsting to kill. I doubted then that we should any of us ever again see the outside of the chapel.

Prayers ended, the priests warned the Indians against committing any excesses and we were allowed to leave the church. The Catholics dipped their fingers in the water at the door and crossed themselves as they passed out. I returned to the shop and the other whites were soon after taken by the Indians back to the agency. King Bird, Big Bear's second son, accompanied me.

"N'Chawamis," he asked, "with whom do you side, Riel or the police?"

"Cousin," I replied, "here we are all friends. The halfbreed war is far from us. Let them fight it out between themselves."

He asked for the loan of the Hudson's Bay Company's flag for the dance he said they intended holding later in the day.

Quinn, cool and self-possessed, his Scotch cap on the back of his head, his hands in his trouser pockets, dropped in on his way to the agency and we spoke together for a few minutes. Leaving, he said to me:

Excerpt from The War Trail of Big Bear, *pp. 66-90, published in 1927 by Small Maynard and Co., of Boston.*

"Well, Cameron, if we come through this alive we'll have something to talk about for the rest of our days."

Wandering Spirit appeared in the door. "Go to the instructor's," he ordered, "where the other whites are!"

I complied. The Indians were sacking the police barracks. As I passed it, Yellow Bear came out, stopping me. Earlier in the day he had asked for a hat, but after thinking a moment had replaced it on the shelf, saying he would get it later. It was now ten o'clock.

"I want to get that hat," he said.

King Bird danced up to me, the Hudson's Bay flag over his shoulders. He shook with suppressed excitement. We had always been good friends.

"N'gowichin! (I'm cold!)" he said. He came closer and added meaningly, in a whisper: "Don't stop around here!"

I turned to Yellow Bear. "You can have the hat," I said. "Come with me."

He hesitated; the old man balked at missing his share of the police plunder. "Won't you bring it to me?" he asked.

"Wandering Spirit has just ordered me here," I answered. "If he saw me going back he might shoot me."

"Very well, then," said Yellow Bear, "I will go with you."

It was not much more than a hundred yards to the shop. Half way we met the war chief. He was running, carrying his rifle at the trail. He stopped and looked at me menacingly. "I thought I told you to stay with the other whites!" he cried.

Yellow Bear answered for me. "He is going with me to get a cap. I have none and the sun is strong."

Wandering Spirit considered. "Hurry back, then!" he said at length, and he ran on.

As I passed the Hudson's Bay house, I saw Big Bear talking with Mrs. Simpson in the kitchen.

Yellow Bear got his cap and I was locking the shop again when Miserable Man appeared with an order from the Indian agent. I glanced across and saw Quinn standing on the hill I had just quitted.

I turned to an old scrapbook and from a piece of foolscap pasted in the back copy the faded lines, the last writing of my brave friend. It is worn and soiled, for I carried it in my waistcoat pocket for many weeks. It is undated, but to me nothing done on that 2nd of April needs a mark. It reads:

"Dear Cameron,
    Please give Miserable Man one blanket.
                                    T.T.Q."

Miserable Man was, I think, the most brutal-looking Indian I have ever seen. His face was deeply pitted by smallpox and the yellow ochre with which it was coated made it appear even more repulsive than usual.

"I have no blankets," I said.

He did not reply, but stood regarding me doubtfully with an ominous look in his rat-like eyes.

"What are you looking at him for?" demanded Yellow Bear. "Don't you hear him say he has no blankets? I know. They have even taken the blankets off his own bed."

Miserable Man was as great a coward as ever breathed. "Well, I suppose I can get something else." Yes, I told him.

"How much?"

"Five dollars."

He selected a shawl, a carrot of tobacco and some tea. I poured the tea into the shawl, as was our custom, and he was tying it up, when a shot rang out a short distance away. It was followed by two more in quick succession.

At the first shot the eyes of Miserable Man opened wide. He caught up the bundle and dashed out of the shop.

I followed, locking the door and putting the heavy brass key in my pocket.

On the hill before the police barracks which I had quitted ten minutes before lay the form of a man. It was the lifeless body of poor Quinn. The air was thick with smoke and dust. It rang with whoops and shrieks and the clatter of galloping hoofs. High over all swelled the deadly war chant of the Plain Crees, bursting from a hundred sinewy throats. I heard Wandering Spirit shout to his followers to shoot the whites, and crack after crack told of the deaths of other of my friends.

"*Atim-eenawuk!* (Dog-men!)" exploded Walking Horse savagely, but half scared, looking out of the Company's house. Big Bear rushed out of the kitchen door and toward his followers, waving his arm and shouting at the top of his voice:

"*Tesqua! Tesqua!* (Stop! Stop!)"

He was too late. The smouldering fire of inherent savagery had burst into flame and he was powerless to quench it; the spring of blood of the old chief's dream had broken forth and spurted through his futile fingers!

My first thought was to seize an axe, lock myself in the house and brain the first man to force the door. But I looked about me and could see no axe. An Indian raced up to me, holding his gun before him.

"If you speak twice, you are a dead man!" he cried.

I saw a halfbreed, Louis Goulet, run past, followed by two Indians. One was his brother-in-law. He was protecting him from the other. Goulet's face was like paper. I turned to Yellow Bear.

"What shall I do?" I asked.

The old man seized my wrist. His hand shook as with the palsy.

"Come this way!" he muttered, dragging me toward the scene of horror. But when he reached the corner of the house, he halted, glanced across and turned back. Big Bear's band had moved during the night and were now camped with the Wood Crees, a mile away. "No!" said Yellow Bear. "These women are starting for the camp. Go with them; do not leave them. They will not shoot among the women!"

Yellow Bear feared openly to befriend me—he would not accompany me—but I did as I was bidden, though I had little hope of reaching the Indian camp. I had gone but a short way when I met the Indian I had seen chasing Goulet. He was riding the halfbreed's white horse, with his rifle across its withers. There was a fence on my right, making it impossible for me to avoid him. I drew back involuntarily, anticipating the worst. He raced up within six feet; then jerked his horse to a sudden stop. He eyed me narrowly for a moment.

"Go on! Go on!" he cried, then. "I don't want to hurt you."

I walked on. Mrs. Simpson looked off to the right in the direction of the firing. She began to tremble violently.

"Oh!" she exclaimed, tears streaming down her face; "the priest has fallen!"

I thought she was about to fall. I stepped back and caught her arm. She pulled away. "Run, white man!" she cried in Cree.

"Do you think they will kill me?"

"Run, white man!" was her only answer.

I walked on. It was useless to run. Death staring me grimly in the face! That was what I saw. Just that. Terrible! I fixed my eyes on the ground before me, held them there determinedly, momentarily expecting the fatal bullet. I did not wish to see when or whence it came. The sooner the better. So I felt. It would be hard for me to describe my feelings in those awful moments of suspense. I was, I believe, resigned. I know I felt that it would be a shame to live when so many of my friends were being foully done to death a few short yards away. I did not even look toward the spot where the tragedy was passing. It seemed that if I did I should be impelled to rush over and fall with my luckless companions. To die without a chance to defend oneself—therein lay the supreme horror! Shot down like a dog! If only I had a gun!

The moments passed. I still lived, and I took heart and raised my eyes at last.

Other armed Indians were running on the ridges nearby. Two passed quite close to me. And at length I reached the camp unharmed. I was told to enter the lodge of a Wood Cree. The women occupying it, all weeping, made tea and gave me a cup. I felt sick and faint.

Soon I heard Wandering Spirit's voice. He was striding up and down through the camp, speaking in his ringing tones:

"*Kapwatamut nipahow!* (I killed the Sioux Speaker!) I met him before the interpreter's house. '*Kapwatamut*,' I said; 'you have a hard head. You boast that when you say no you mean no. Today, if you love your life, you will do as I tell you. Go to our camp.'

" 'Why should I go there?' he demanded.

" 'Never mind,' I said. 'Go.'

" 'My place is here,' he answered. 'Big Bear has not asked me to leave. I will not go.'

"I raised my rifle. 'I tell you—*go!*' I shouted, and I shot him dead."

Three Indians entered the lodge and sat down near me. They looked at me curiously. I knew them well, but I did not speak. They had watches belonging to the murdered men. One, Papamakeesik, Père Fafard's murderer, held out a watch and asked me the time. It was eleven o'clock.

I groaned, sitting there, thinking over the horror. I expected each moment they would come for me. The suspense became unendurable. I could not longer rest with my fate undecided; I must go out! I told these Indians. They were friendly enough to suggest that I disguise myself in a blanket, but I said no. I might be recognized. If I were I should be shot on suspicion of attempting to escape.

I walked across the camp into the brush. William Gladieu, the Wood Cree who had befriended me in the morning, followed with his gun. He put his arm about my shoulders.

"My brother," he exclaimed, "you are not to be killed. Before that happens they will walk over my dead body. Come."

He took me to the tent of *Oneepohayo*, head chief of the Wood Crees. Here a council was assembled. Yellow Bear, Little Bear, Gladieu and others, including the chief himself, spoke of kindnesses received at my hands—trifles as they seemed at the time, but which were to stand me in good stead now. They agreed that I should live and left me to secure Wandering Spirit's consent.

The Plain Crees were in council outside and the war chief made a speech to the band, instructing them that I was not to be harmed. They brought him to the lodge.

"This is the young man whose life we ask," said Chief *Oneepohayo*.

"Ah-ha!" answered the war chief. "He has done me favours too." He held out his hand.

Can anyone realize how sweet life really is until he comes near to losing it? I doubt it. Mine, I began to think, might still be endurable—worth an effort to save. Though my spirit revolted I took the hand that had sped the bullets that sent two of my companions to a sudden and awful end, for besides the agent he had shot one of the priests.

"Walk about during the day as you please," he said, "but don't go out at night. You might be shot. One of the young men might do it and we wouldn't know who. And don't try to escape."

At Cold Lake, forty miles to the north, H. R. Halpin was in charge of the Hudson's Bay Company's post. A party was leaving to bring him to Frog Lake. I took advantage of their amiable mood to put in a word for him.

"Promise you'll spare his life, also," I urged. They debated the matter and made the promise. "So that he won't be surprised, I'll give you a note for him," I said, and on the back of an envelope I wrote in pencil:

> Dear Halpin,
> The Crees have murdered every white man here except myself. They are going out for you and have promised not to harm you. At your peril, offer no resistance.

Beverley Robertson, the lawyer who defended the Indians, had this note at the time of the trial, but I do not know where it is now.

Toward evening James K. Simpson arrived from Pitt. He was an old officer of the Hudson's Bay Company, with supervision over several posts and headquarters at Frog Lake, where I lived with him. As he drove into camp the Indians stopped his horses, unharnessed and appropriated them. He was an old friend of Big Bear and although a white man, in no great danger, for his halfbreed wife had two sons members of the Wood Cree bands.

"Big Bear," said Mr. Simpson before the whole band, "I have known you for twenty-five years and I never thought I should live to see a thing like this!"

There was deep feeling in the old chief's voice as he answered sorrowfully: "It is not my work. They have tried for a long time to take away my good name and they have done it at last. If you had been here, this might never have happened."

Mr. Simpson was allowed his own tent, while I was lodged with one of his stepsons, Louis Patenaude. I was deadly weary, and with the boastful jests of the murderers in my ears, lay down early and slept that night as soundly as ever I did in my life. It was a blessed relief to be able to forget in sleep the appalling events of that day.

These were the first hours of my memorable two months with hostile Indians.

I may here appropriately mention the fact that no servant of the Hudson's Bay Company was killed by the Indians during the whole of this stormy period. Their treatment by the Company had always been considerate and humane. If an Indian was sick he went to the nearest post and was supplied with food and medicine until he became well. When ready to go on a hunt he was outfitted with provisions, traps and ammunition, for which he paid in furs on his return. The Company made him advances in goods on account of his annuity and waited almost a year for payment, trusting entirely to his honesty for settlement of the debt. After a trade he always got a small present. When hungry he was never denied a meal.

It was this policy of liberality that created the bond of friendship that existed between the red men and the Company for more than two hundred years and of which they were not forgetful even in their moment of savage vengeance.

Yet the fact that I was an employee of the Hudson's Bay Company would not alone have saved me in that awful hour, and I cannot conclude this story of the massacre without recording here the sense of deep gratitude I shall always feel for life preserved under circumstances I can never cease to regard as anything but miraculous.

Nine men were killed in the massacre:

Thomas Trueman Quinn, a native of Minnesota, thirty-eight years of age, of mixed Irish, French and Sioux blood, successively interpreter, clerk and agent in the Canadian Indian service.

John Delaney, farming instructor, a native of Ontario, about forty years of age.

John C. Gowanlock, from Parkdale, Ontario, about twenty-eight years of age.

George Dill, about forty years of age. He came from Muskoka, Ontario, to Frog Lake in the fall before the massacre as my partner in a trading business.

John Williscraft came to the West from Southampton, Ontario. He was a mechanic, about sixty years of age.

William C. Gilchrist, clerk for Mr. Gowanlock, about twenty-one years of age.

Charles Gouin, a Columbia River halfbreed, employed at Frog Lake building the agency stores and houses. He was about forty years of age.

Rev. Leon Adelard Fafard, a native of Quebec, where he was born in 1849.

Rev. Felix Marie Marchand was born in France in 1858.

Another Death Threat

The council sat on the grass in a circle, a triple row of painted and befeathered savages. They made a way for me to reach the hollow space in the centre, and Wandering Spirit, who sat on his heels inside the inner row, motioned me to sit beside him on the right. He wore his war bonnet and a rifle rested across his knees. From the bonnet depended five broad white eagle plumes, their points jet-tipped, for each of which I had heard him boast he meant to have a white man's life. Until then he had taken just two, those of Quinn and Father Marchand, so that three were still needed to make good his boast.

Immediately behind Wandering Spirit sat Imasees, half-brother to King Bird. Imasees was the real instigator of the Frog Lake atrocities, though clever enough so to manoeuvre that upon others should fall the blame. He was emphatically a dangerous Indian—a cool, commanding figure in the flush of young manhood, with muscles of spring steel and the features of a Roman legionary. He wore his hair roached above his unwinking black eyes, like a horse's foretop, and he had about him something of the dominating force which despite his age still remained to Big Bear. In fact, so striking an example of the pure type of Plains savage was Imasees that notwithstanding his crafty and treacherous nature, I could not but confess a degree of secret admiration for him.

John Pritchard sat in the centre of the hollow space, with Mr. Simpson beside him. I noticed Fitzpatrick sitting with some halfbreeds, including Andre Nault, Louis Goulet and Abram Montour, on the left of the circle. Louis Patenaude, my guard in

Excerpt from The War Trail of Big Bear, *pp. 88-99, published in 1927 by Small Maynard and Co., of Boston.*

camp, and Alexis Crossarms, sat immediately beside Wandering Spirit on the left; William Gladieu on his right. The Plain Crees completely surrounded us. As I walked to the place assigned me and glanced over the banked ring of bedaubed and forbidding faces, a sense of the peril which hemmed us in came upon me. Should we ever again pass that barrier of sinister faces? I tried to tell myself that we should, but it was not easy.

Wandering Spirit fixed me with the eyes that always seemed to bore into one's very soul and raising a hand as if to impress me with the importance of what he had to say, he began:

"You are one of them, the big Company. You trade with the Crees for furs and write everything down in a book. Tell me—you know: The Company sold this land to the Big Chief Woman; took money for it. Why did they do that? This land belongs to us. The Company did not own it. But they are rich because they got much money for something that was not theirs. We are not rich. We are poor. Often we do not have enough to eat. So we have taken back the land, and when it is sold again—to the Long Knives (Americans)—the money will come to us, not to the Company.

"You saw what happened the other day; how Sioux Speaker and those other men dropped. It is *iyamun* when the Crees make war! Plenty blood runs. This, that began the other day—it will go on until there are no longer any Canadians here. That was my vow when I fired the first shot. Now, say: Why did they sell the land? How much did they get?"

I realized the need for carefully considered replies to any questions he might put to me. I was in no hurry to answer. Wandering Spirit, backed no doubt by Imasees, had set a trap for me. I was the only living white man who had witnessed the butchery at Frog Lake. It gave him, I think, a sense of uneasiness when he looked at me and recalled that. It was an omen of bad luck. Wandering Spirit had never forgiven me, I knew, for being still alive and I had no doubt his mind was made up, notwithstanding his professions of good will, to remedy the miscarriage of his designs and dispose of me at the earliest opportunity. That might arise at any instant with a hasty slip of my tongue.

Wandering Spirit knew no English and our conversation was carried on in Cree.

"I do not carry all these things in my head," I said at length, "but I will try to tell you. The Hudson's Bay Company did not sell the country; as you say, it was not theirs to sell. But the Great Mother thought they had some rights. They had been here two hundred years. That is a long time. If you had lived for two

hundred years on a piece of land you would be very bitter if
somebody took it away. The Queen made a treaty with the
Indians and the Hudson's Bay Company had to give up the
land—most of it. They could not be driven out—or where would
the Indians have traded their furs?—and they had to live
somewhere; they had to have land for their posts. Now, you ask
why the Great Mother paid money to the Company. I will tell you.
The Company had been good to the Indians, so the Great Mother,
when she sent her money chiefs to make the treaty, paid the
Company three hundred thousand pounds."

Wandering Spirit clapped his hands over his mouth in the Cree
gesture of astonishment too colossal for expression in words.
Then he swung suddenly upon me and said in his peculiarly
penetrative tones:

"You knew about the fighting at Duck Lake—knew before the
bad day here. If you Company men were friends of the Crees, you
would have told the news. You told us nothing."

The fight, between Riel and the North-West Mounted Police,
occurred on March 26th; we had learned of it five days later. Frog
Lake followed on April 2nd. This was April 4th. We had not
thought it wise to say anything to the Indians about the rising at
Duck Lake.

I said: "I overheard something of your talk. You knew all about
it—more than we did. I could not tell you anything."

"Well, we will see how much you know now," he persisted.
"Tell me all about it—the halfbreed war; how it started, who were
killed, how many soldiers, where they are. Speak with one
tongue."

He had given me a formidable and disturbing task. "Mr.
Simpson brought me a *musinagan* from Pitt. It tells about Duck
Lake—the fighting. I will get the paper and read it to you." I rose,
but he stopped me with a gesture.

"If you saw it, you know what it says. You don't need the
paper."

My position had now reached a point of extreme difficulty and
danger. I could not rely on memory to give him exact details of the
battle or of the movements and numbers of troops—already on
their way from the East to the Saskatchewan. Yet there were
halfbreeds in the camp able to read English and I knew that the
paper would be taken and read by one of them following this
examination and that any trifling discrepancy would be seized on
by Wandering Spirit to fix upon me a charge of falsehood and
attempt to mislead the band. A pretext to denounce me as an

enemy of the Crees was all that was wanted by Wandering Spirit.

"You must think me very wise, *Kahpaypamahchakwayo*," I replied. "I am not so clever. You do not make it easy for me; you make it hard." I looked round at the rows of tense, unsmiling faces. Some of them, I knew, were my friends.

"Hear—I am speaking to the council—I want to say, I will tell all I remember! If I leave anything out that is in the paper—if I do not tell something exactly as it is there—do not say I spoke with two tongues. That will not be so!" A shout of the approving *"How!"* ran round the circle. I went on:

"The South Branch halfbreeds, misled by Riel and other headmen, threatened to seize the traders' stores at Duck Lake. The chief of the Mounted Police, with fifty men, on the way from Fort Carlton to Duck Lake to protect the stores, met the halfbreeds under Riel and Dumont and a battle followed. Eleven of the white men were killed; some wounded. Some of the halfbreeds and a few of Beardy's Crees, also. A bullet ploughed through Gabriel Dumont's scalp; the white chief was wounded in the face. The police had returned to Carlton. The head chief of the Mounted Police had arrived there with one hundred more men, but he had burned Fort Carlton and moved down to Prince Albert. One of the Queen's big soldier chiefs had reached the Touchwood Hills with two thousand men. More soldiers were following from Red River. An——"

"I don't believe all this!" Wandering Spirit broke in excitedly. "Liar!"

I looked him in the eye. "You asked me to tell you what the paper says. I am telling you. I don't know whether it's true or not. Some things I am not very sure about. But about the soldiers—I remember that."

"You seem to remember everything against us—all this talk of soldiers coming to fight us," he sneered. He regarded me darkly for a moment; then: "I am going to ask another question. A minute ago you wanted everyone to hear you. Let them hear you now when you answer: Do you want to see Riel win, or the whites? Whose side are you on?"

I hope never again to find myself in so critical a predicament. I could not bring myself, in no matter what extremity, to say I sided with these cut-throats, even though, because the thought of death so appalled me just then, I had taken the hand held out to me by the arch-assassin when he promised on the demand of *Oneepohayo* that I should not be harmed—that lean, claw-like hand the closing of which half an hour before had loosed the ball that stretched poor Quinn dead at his feet.

What I finally did say—and I spoke to the whole council—was:

"The other day you made us—ten white men—prisoners, over yonder. A little later nine died. I am glad that I am alive—that you saved me—but I have no life of my own any more. It is yours. I am in your camp. Who can I side with?"

I was manoeuvring to avoid stating a deliberate falsehood but the effect to me was startling. I had looked for quick manifestations of anger over an evasive answer. What I met was a chorus of approval of my reply. In brief, I had made a hit. But not with Wandering Spirit. Of that his face was the unspoken evidence.

I took advantage of a temporary lull in events to move, with the air of regarding my position in the camp as definitely established, to a seat in the open space near Pritchard, about six feet in front of Wandering Spirit. But a moment later he turned on me again and said sharply:

"Say that you will stay with the Crees—will help them, not try to get away!"

I nodded.

I could see his eyes kindle as he looked off to the right for a second; then he faced me again: "Swear it!" he commanded. "Raise your hand!"

But the sympathy of many in the council had by this swung over to me. They shouted "He did swear!"

"Namoya!" retorted the war chief angrily. "He did not!"

A clamour of virulent dispute arose, my champions asserting loudly that I had sworn, most of Big Bear's men as vociferously combating the statement. The war of words mounted to an uproar, till at length Wandering Spirit, fearing an actual clash between the two factions, Wood and Plain Crees, dropped the point and I escaped taking the hateful oath.

I have many times thought over the occurrence and long ago reached the conclusion that what followed was just one detail, worked out probably by Imasees or by Imasees and Wandering Spirit together, in the game these two master conspirators had set out to play.

I question if, barring Big Bear himself and his son-in-law, The Lone Man—perhaps the bravest redskin I ever knew—there was in that whole camp of two hundred lodges a single Indian who was not afraid of Wandering Spirit. I do not except even Imasees, truculent by nature though he was. The Lone Man and the war chief hated each other with a deadly enmity, but—because of that no doubt—they also avoided one another, contact spelling danger for both. No brave in his right mind who wished to continue living would deliberately have provoked Wandering Spirit.

Oseewoosgwan—Bald Head—was very old and he had the mind of a very old man. That is why I put him down a tool of Imasees. From his actions and appearance I am certain no sense of danger entered his shrunken old brain as, leaning heavily on a stick, he pushed his way into the circle and bending over, with a finger pointed derisively at the war chief, piped in a high querulous falsetto:

"For what do you keep these white people here? You did not hold back the other day." He waved a hand in the direction of the smoking desolation. "But now you talk—just talk. You have done bad already. It beats you to go on with what you started, eh?"

The blood surged to Wandering Spirit's face, flushing it darkly, as he sat looking up from beneath his war bonnet at the old man. Suddenly his right hand shot out, throwing the lever of his Winchester down in the action of loading and thereby raising the muzzle.

He jumped to his feet. "You will see today whether it beats me!" he shouted.

But rapid as had been his movements, Louis Patenaude and Alexis Crossarms had anticipated them. They were both on their feet at his left; in one hand Louis grasped the barrel of the Winchester and held it above his head; behind, Alexis reinforced his hold with a double grip of his own on the gun. Any effort by the now infuriated leader to control the weapon was effectually blocked. In vain he struggled to lower the barrel, to raise the butt to his shoulder. Alexis and Louis held the Winchester as in a vice.

I had leaped to my feet at the first move of the war chief and now stood with muscles tensed, oblivious to everything else, watching with fascinated interest the drama being played out before me. How would it end? If the maddened war chief succeeded by any chance in wresting the gun from my defenders I was ready to throw myself upon him and seize the rifle before he could level and discharge it at me. At Frog Lake I had walked along while rifles cracked and screams and whoops and war cries a hundred yards away made a stunning horror of the golden April morning, weaponless, like a man with hands bound, my eyes on the ground before me, expecting each instant a bullet in the back. Here at least there was certainty of action. I would go down, if it was my fate, fighting—I hoped with a kind of wild joy, bringing others down with me—not like a dog! I was too engrossed at the moment to feel any sense of fear.

A long knife stuck in a sheath in Wandering Spirit's belt. Both the war chief's hands were engaged with his gun. Patenaude bent forward suddenly and with his right hand plucked the knife from the sheath and raising his arm, held the point poised an inch above Wandering Spirit's heart. Then he craned forward until his face almost met that of the war chief and with eyes that glittered under the black brows like a snake's, bent upon the eyes opposing them a look of such calculated deadliness that in the hush that fell upon the staring council only the subdued clicking of stealthily-lifted gun hammers could be heard.

The war chief's fury died under the menace of those level eyes, and over the copper features spread a film of dull grey, like dusted ashes. But he still fought, though without his former desperate recklessness, for possession of the Winchester.

Gladieu had risen with Wandering Spirit and his gun was now levelled on the war chief's head from behind. The hilt of the knife protruded above Louis' hand. Imasees, who had also risen and stood at Wandering Spirit's back, reached under his shoulder, grasped the protruding handle and with a sudden jerk drew the knife through, leaving an ugly gash across Louis' fingers. Then Imasees, with outstretched arms and the naked blade in his left hand flashing in the sun, glanced quickly round the circle and spoke, in low, emotionless tones:

"This is not the way to do! It will make trouble between us. We want to be all friends!"

The way of retreat had been opened for Wandering Spirit. He seized it eagerly—no doubt gratefully.

"*Uh-huh!*" he exclaimed, his head nodding to emphasize his agreement. "*Tapwa!* (True!) The old man's talk made my heart bad, but that is past. We are all Crees here, all brothers!"

Alexis and Louis had kept their hold on the rifle, but when Wandering Spirit lowered the hammer they released it. Gladieu stepped over, pushed his shoulder against that of the war chief and his rifle alongside the Winchester and watched narrowly while the two guns came down together. The significance of Gladieu's action lay in the fact that he distrusted the war chief's professed change of heart. He was guarding against a feint—a surprise by Wandering Spirit once control of his Winchester had passed again into his own hands.

Wandering Spirit was seated once more, but I still stood, absorbed as ever, awaiting the next development. He looked up presently and motioned with his hand.

"Apee!" he said. *"Sit! Numanando keeah!"* For which there is no adequate translation. What he meant to convey was that I was not in danger at the moment. Which was satisfactory as far as it went.

The strain had proved too much for the war chief and as he sat before me I noted the violent shaking of his hands and knees, which he sought in vain to control. The depression that had come over him he was unable to throw off and in a few minutes he had left the circle and the council was over.

Big Bear stopped me on my way back to Patenaude's lodge.

"Okemasis," said the chief, "you were foolish to stand up just now. Any could have shot you without danger to the others. Sitting you were safer."

I saw the force of Big Bear's statement. Pritchard said: "How did you ever get up? I could not have moved to save my life. They could have knocked me on the head like a rabbit."

Fitzpatrick had tried to rise, but Big Bear, who sat behind him, pulled him down. So the old chief not only preached common sense; he put it into practice.

I was walking through the camp a day or two later. The drummers were beating the big drum; the war song rose above the assembled braves. I glanced over at the group and gasped. Two warriors shuffled up and down in the war dance, over their shoulders the gilt and white vestments of their most unworldly and inoffensive victims, the dead priests. I was not a Roman Catholic, but apart from its, for me, poignant personal significance, the sight so completely outraged those feelings of reverence I had been brought up to entertain for all things sacred that I could only stand and stare. It remains among my most vivid impressions of that terrible two months.

Big Bear's Trial Speech

I was a witness at the trial of Big Bear, giving evidence for the defence. I told how, at the moment of the shooting he had rushed toward the murderers shouting: *"Tesqua! Tesqua!* (Stop! Stop!),*"* how he had expressed to Mr. Simpson his sorrow for what had occurred, how at our suggestion he had called a council to urge his followers to let the police quit Fort Pitt unmolested, and had afterward held his band back when Captain Dickens abandoned the place, how he had spoken for us when Wandering Spirit in council tried to incite a second massacre, how *Chaquapocase* (as I learned) the night after Frenchman's Butte had started for the McLeans' tent to shoot the chief trader in revenge for the death of the murderer *Kahweechetwaymot* and how Big Bear had gone after him and taken away his gun.

The old chief was in sore perplexity and distress and I spoke fervently in his behalf. With a world of trouble in the kindly expressive old eyes he sat and watched me while the interpreter beside him translated my testimony in his ear, and as I warmed in his defence and the words came fast and tumultuously to my lips he nodded his head emphatically in confirmation and the cloud seemed to lift from his seamed and rugged patriarchal face. Big Bear is dead, but it will always be a source of gratification to me that I had the opportunity of doing something to lighten the misfortunes that overtook his old age and that I made the most of it.

The charge was treason-felony and the verdict guilty. Brought before the court to learn his fate, Justice Richardson said:

"Big Bear, have you anything to say before sentence is passed upon you?"

Excerpt from The War Trail of Big Bear, *pp. 221-225, published in 1927 by Small Maynard and Co., of Boston.*

The old man drew himself up with that imperious air that proclaimed him leader and fitted him so well; the thick nostrils expanded, the broad deep chest was thrown out, the strong jaw looked aggressively prominent, the mouth was a straight line. He gave his head the little characteristic toss that always preceded his speeches.

"I think I should have something to say," he began slowly, "about the occurrences which brought me here in chains!" He spoke in his native Cree, knowing no English. He paused. Then with the earnestness, the eloquence and the pathos that never failed to move an audience, red or white, he went on to speak of the troubles of the spring.

"I knew little of the killing at Frog Lake beyond hearing shots fired. When any wrong was brewing I did my best to stop it in the beginning. The turbulent ones of the band got beyond my control and shed the blood of those I would have protected. I was away from Frog Lake a part of the winter, hunting and fishing, and the rebellion had commenced before I got back. When white men were few in the country I gave them the hand of brotherhood. I am sorry so few are here who can witness for my friendly acts.

"Can anyone stand out and say that I ordered the death of a priest or an agent? You think I encouraged my people to take part in the trouble. I did not. I advised them against it. I felt sorry when they killed those men at Frog Lake, but the truth is when news of the fight at Duck Lake reached us my band ignored my authority and despised me because I did not side with the halfbreeds. I did not so much as take a white man's horse. I always believed that by being the friend of the white man, I and my people would be helped by those of them who had wealth. I always thought it paid to do all the good I could. Now my heart is on the ground.

"I look around me in this room and see it crowded with handsome faces—faces far handsomer than my own (Laughter). I have ruled my country for a long time. Now I am in chains and will be sent to prison, but I have no doubt the handsome faces I admire about me will be competent to govern the land (Laughter). At present I am as dead to my people. Many of my band are hiding in the woods, paralyzed with terror. Cannot this court send them a pardon? My own children!—perhaps they are starving and outcast, too, afraid to appear in the big light of day. If the government does not come to them with help before the winter sets in, my band will surely perish.

"But I have too much confidence in the Great Grandmother to fear that starvation will be allowed to overtake my people. The time will come when the Indians of the North-West will be of much service to the Great Grandmother. I plead again to you, the chiefs of the white men's laws, for pity and help to the outcasts of my band!

"I have only a few words more to say. Sometimes in the past I have spoken stiffly to the Indian agents, but when I did so it was only in order to obtain my rights. The North-West belonged to me, but I perhaps will not live to see it again. I ask the court to publish my speech and to scatter it among the white people. It is my defence.

"I am old and ugly, but I have tried to do good. Pity the children of my tribe! Pity the old and the helpless of my people! I speak with a single tongue; and because Big Bear has always been the friend of the white man, send out and pardon and give them help!

"*How! Aquisanee*—I have spoken!"

A tense silence held the crowded courtroom as Big Bear concluded. The man would have been calloused indeed who could listen to that stirring appeal, the impassioned outburst of the aged, untutored orator, unmoved. The fates had been unkind. Dejected he was, lonely, shorn of his freedom, bewildered he must have been. But however broken he might be, and probably was in the privacy of his solitary cell, here, before the people of an alien race who had entered and possessed his land, he was still able to hold up his head; he was still Big Bear, chief of the Crees. The stout old heart still beat strongly in the warrior breast. His spirit, though bowed, refused to be crushed. And his plea was—not for himself; he was above that—but for his people, far less worthy than himself—for his children, hiding in terror, "afraid to show themselves in the big light of day." My eyes—I am not ashamed to say it—were wet. My heart went out to the kindly, pleasant old man I had known, who found "so few to witness for his friendly acts." I was glad not to be among that absent number.

"Big Bear," said Justice Richardson, and his tone was not unkind, "you have been found guilty by an impartial jury. You cannot be excused from all responsibility for the misdoings of your band. The sentence of the court is that you be imprisoned in the penitentiary at Stony Mountain for three years."

The Fall of Stalking Spirit
(Fiction)

It was long since the Plain Crees had done any fighting, and they seemed to be enjoying the prospect of a little. In the years of peaceful quiet that had followed the advent of the Redcoats, they had hugged their weapons and thought on the past—on the days when they lived by the buffalo, stole horses, traded for whiskey, drank themselves drunk, fought the Blackfoot, slew, lost scalps, and were altogether happy—and the martial spark died not, but smouldered. And now a light wind of insurrection had touched it and it had flashed suddenly into flame.

With the Wood Crees it was different. Primarily fur hunters in the timbered north, they had ventured seldom onto the plains among their warlike brethren and the implacable Blackfoot, and had acquired little of their love of conflict. Yet, with less than half their numbers, but with better arms, Big Wolf's Plain Cree band ruled the camp and had threatened and coerced them into an alliance against the whites, with whom they had no quarrel. A month before, this cut-throat band, under the war chief, Stalking

Reprinted from Northwest Magazine, *St. Paul, Minn., May 1898. This fictional account is based on the events described in "Another Death Threat." Actual names of persons and places mentioned in the story are: Stalking Spirit (Wandering Spirit), Big Wolf (Chief Big Bear), Lampson (Simpson of HBC), Tall Pine (Louis Patenaude), Chief One Hand (Woodland Cree chief Cut Arm), Ohskatask (Ohskatask), General Odds (General Strange, of Alberta Field Force), Singing Lake (Frog Lake), and Fort Marais (Fort Pitt). Jim Vue was a fictional creation as, no doubt, was the maiden Soft Hair. Bellwood, the clerk, is Cameron himself. In real life, Wandering Spirit did attempt to commit suicide and was later executed; the rift between the Woodland and Plains Cree also is accurately described, but there was no internal uprising.*

Spirit, had risen one morning at dawn and treacherously murdered all the white men in the little outpost of Singing Lake. The settlers in the surrounding country had flocked to the barracks at Fort Marais, which the Indians attacked. The garrison detachment abandoned the fort and went down the Saskatchewan in a scow, the refugees came into the camp under the assurance of protection given by the Wood Crees, and now the red man once more roved supreme in the land of his fathers and his gods.

But in making prisoners they also made a mistake, and the Plain Crees have since declared that, should they ever again take the war trail, they will make no more captives.

On a bright, warm afternoon in May, Big Wolf's band danced the war dance. A few of the prisoners lounged among the Wood Crees, looking on. The dancers marched in a body around the great circle formed by the two hundred tents, dancing before the lodges of the head men. Sometimes they squatted on the ground to rest, in a small circle of their own.

"Not a great many of 'em, is there?" remarked Jim Vue to a little, gray-bearded man beside him. Jim and his string team had happened to be at Fort Marais when it fell. Stalking Spirit now paraded the camp on his gray lead mare, her sides and flanks gay with vermilion and white mud, a bunch of feathers floating from her foretop. Four Sky Thunder rode the other leader. The rest of his horses were distributed among the band.

"Many!" returned the graybeard in a tone of disgust. "Why, I've known six white men chase a bigger crowd clear over a cutbank into a canyon, in old days. There's more than enough Wood Indians to herd 'em all into inferno with a rush, if they only had the sand." He was an old servant of the Hudson's Bay Company, named Lampson. Big Wolf's band had attached his horses, also, and he felt sore.

Jim Vue mused for a moment, with his dark eyes on the grass.

"Say! there's a great proposition," he said, at length, in a low tone. "Suppose we try to work a scheme? I'd like to have a hand in a little game o' that sort myself. There's been too much of a sameness in this camp to suit me durin' the two weeks I've been in it; a little, just a little riffle would do a feller good—wake him up, an' start his blood movin' again. Now, see here, we'll take Bellwood, the clerk—he knows enough to keep a grip on his tongue—an' Fitz an' one or two others, maybe—ask 'em to sit in, an' we'll work a scheme; yes, we'll work a scheme. What d' y'u say, uncle?" he concluded, turning upon the old man eyes lighted with the sparkle of daring and pleasurable anticipation, and with a smile at the corners of his mouth.

"Why, I'm with you," responded old Lampson, heartily. "But we've got to be cautious. We can't be too cautious," he repeated. "If Big Wolf's crowd got just an echo of this, we might say by-bye to our locks; they would never grow any more. Not that I have many to lose, but such as they are——" He laughed a little asthmatic laugh, stroking his thin beard tenderly. "It'll take time, though," he added, "a week, anyway."

Stalking Spirit arose. He had been sitting on his feet at the head of the circle, digging in the turf with his long, keen hunting knife and watching the captives. He threw his rifle over his arm and strode rapidly up and down opposite them.

"When I commenced this thing yonder," he began in that soft, ringing voice which always made his hearers think of the panther, "I made a vow that I would never look upon a white man except to kill him. Now I look about me in the camp and see white faces everywhere. They begin to group together and talk, and the first thing we know one will get away and bring trouble upon us. It's not the halfbreeds I mean; they're our friends, our relations. It's these white people I'm talking about!"

He leaned forward and indicated Jim Vue and the others with a sweep of his arm. The eyes of the young bucks grew bright and ominous-looking as he spoke. Some who had left their guns stole off to their lodges and returned with them. Several halfbreeds sat among the whites. They edged silently away until not one was within two paces. Tall Pine, a warrior of big Wolf's band, slipped around and stretched himself on the grass behind the clerk, who had helped him when he had been starving in the winter. He grasped Bellwood's hand and pressed it.

"My brother!" he said softly, in the Cree tongue, smiling.

Bellwood was touched. It meant that he, Tall Pine, at least, would defend him while breath remained in his stiff, worn old body.

"I pity every white man that has been saved," said the old head chief, Big Wolf, tremulously, rising and holding forth his hands toward the prisoners. "Instead of speaking bad, you should give back some of their things. They are half naked. Let your hearts be soft toward them."

Bald Head approached, and, pointing a scornful finger at the war chief, spoke in mocking tones:

"Why do you still look upon white faces and waste time in talk when you say you made a vow? You do bad, and then it beats you to go on with what you began!"

Stalking Spirit sprang to his feet. "You will see today if it beats me!" he shouted angrily, pumping a cartridge into his Winchester. Tall Pine and a Wood Cree leaped at the muzzle of the menacing rifle and stayed it above their heads. Another Wood Cree leveled his gun on the war chief from behind. With one hand Tall Pine reached over and plucked the knife from Stalking Spirit's own belt. He held the point before the leader's heart and, with head thrown forward, fixed him with a gleaming eye. The head soldier quailed under that deadly glance. His arms began to tremble. Little Wicked jumped up behind the war chief. He stealthily put his hand forward and snatched the knife through Tall Pine's fingers. Then he stood with the naked blade pointed from him, flashing in the sun, and spoke quickly:

"This is not the way to do. It will make trouble between us. We want to be all friends."

The way of retreat had been opened for Stalking Spirit, and he availed himself of it eagerly, thankfully.

"*Aha! Tapwa!*" he assented, grounding his rifle. "I was angry. The old man made me mad. It is over; it is nothing."

He sat again. But his knees continued to shake as with a palsy. He did not dance more, and the drum that afternoon soon ceased to beat.

Jim Vue sauntered off whistling, with his hands in his pockets. The prisoners were allowed to walk unattended about the camp during the day, but were warned that the escape of one meant death to the others. An hour later a select council of four was in session on the confines of the camp. It sat under the broad canopy of heaven and far enough from the nearest lodge to be safely out of earshot of any of the dusky inmates. Jim was unfolding his proposition, while the others craned forward with eyes and ears intent.

"Easy as eatin' breakfast," he was saying—"which I just forgot, for a minute, ain't always the easiest thing, here. But take Big Wolf's outfit when they're dancin'. They're all in a bunch, like a band o' sheep, then; nobody to home 'cept the women an' children. We set the Wood Crees on, One Hand, the chief, to lead. Each has his man picked, an' they're standin' around, same's ordinary, with the Plain Crees sittin' in a little coil on the ground. All of a sudden One Hand holds up his stump—*whoof!* a volley—an' where's your Plain Crees? Ain't they devilish enough to deserve it?" he went on in a sort of a whine, like a maddened hound ready to spring at the throat of a tormentor. "Have we been safe any time? Are we safe now, any minute? I reckon not, if there's no objection. See this afternoon!"

"God's truth!" exclaimed Bellwood. "Hanging 'ud be too good for them, after the way they took those poor fellows unawares at the Lake. Give 'em a hot, swift dose of their own pills, I say!"

"Nobody'll dispute your argument on the safety question, Jim," put in Fitzmorris. "Why, I can see that they hate the very sight of me, every time I stroll through the camp."

"Then it's settled. Only, as our uncle, here, says, we must be careful; we can't be too careful. If the Plain Crees got just a breath—well, I guess it ain't necessary to go into particulars with you fellers," concluded Jim; and the session ended.

The next afternoon Jim Vue, with Lampson as interpreter, held confidential speech with One Hand. The chief's daughter, Soft Hair, listened, like Desdemona to Othello, while Jim unfolded his plans. At length he paused and looked earnestly at the chief, who, after some deliberation, replied:

"Your words are very pleasant in my ears, O my brother and friend! It was not our wish to lift our arms against the white man. These murderers forced our young men to it—and see how they treat us now! They take our horses, as they have taken yours, and kill our cattle. With bragging they rule the camp. They are not braver—no, not so brave as our own young men; but these are like whipped dogs. Yet wait; we shall see if they are able to do as they have. Meanwhile—peace."

Never had Soft Hair seen anyone like this dark Westerner—with his daring and experiences, his light-heartedness. His words, she thought, sounded like the sighing of summer winds; his swift, bright glances seemed as the odour of the pines. She was bound to him as with thongs of deerskin; she would do anything in her power to please Not Afraid, the white man. Jim was not especially fond of her; for, how could he so soon forget? No matter. Perhaps *Minnishooshay* had herself forgotten, ere this. At all events, he liked Soft Hair well enough, and, like any other true son of the ample West, he was never entirely happy unless he had "a girl."

Here was Soft Hair's chance. He did not give her all his heart. She would further his plans, the plans he urged upon her father. Then he would know how she loved him, and she would make him love her and her alone. Yet, if he were killed in the fight probably to follow? Better that, than that he should leave her for another; but she would not think of it.

An uneventful fortnight passed. Jim was disgusted. He declared that in another ten such days he should die of sheer inaction. The Wood Crees had not been brought to the sticking point; they apparently lacked courage. "Wait!" was all the reply he was able to wrest from One Hand, when he complained with bitterness to him of the delay.

Then, most unexpectedly, occurred an incident which set the ball going rapidly. The hitch had been here: Stalking Spirit had divined that a rupture was imminent between his followers and their brethren of the Wood, that these harboured a feeling of resentment at the high-handed way in which his men had been carrying affairs. Consequently, he had hastened to adopt a conciliatory attitude and had been doing all he could to engender sentiments more fraternal between the factions. In this he was in a measure successful; he had stayed, from day to day, the hour of retribution.

Ohskatask was an Indian of Big Wolf's band. One morning, when the camp lay some miles from Fort Marais, a number of the Plain Crees went to fetch some flour and bacon which had been left there by the garrison. Gladieu, the halfbreed, had a wife from among the Wood Crees. He sat on the ground before his tent in the Wood Cree camp, holding by a line a fine roam mare, when *Ohskatask* walked up to him.

"Lend me your mare," said the Indian. "I wish to go to the fort."

The halfbreed knew that if he lent her she would not be returned.

"Borrow from your own people, *Ohskatask*," he answered. "I have use for my horse."

"*Muchastim!*" muttered the Indian, jamming the muzzle of his rifle into the halfbreed's eye, and snatching the line out of his hand, he jumped on the mare and rode off.

Stalking Spirit witnessed this. In his new role of peacemaker, he went after his unruly follower, calling upon him to stop. *Ohskatask* faced about, and the two Indians—the one sullen, defiant, the other wrathful, threatening—with fingers on the locks of their guns, glared at one another for a moment from beneath their war bonnets.

"*Fool!*" hissed Stalking Spirit. "Do you wish to bring us into war with these weak-kneed Wood Indians? Give up the mare. We are not strong enough to hold our power if they once will fight."

"I only borrowed her," said the other, doggedly. "He can have her when I get back."

"I have not been slow to kill a man that vexes or opposes me," said the war chief, scornfully. "Give up the mare, *Keesquayon!*"

"I will return her—after," reiterated *Ohskatask*. He wheeled suddenly and, with an eye back over his shoulder, beat his heels against his horse's ribs and clattered away toward the fort.

"A bad fool," said Stalking Spirit to the Wood Crees. "I can do nothing, unless I killed him, and that I had rather not." He returned to his own side of the camp. *Ohskatask* had his friends in Big Wolf's band, and this may not have been without his influence on the war chief's disposition.

Five minutes later, one of One Hand's young men rode swiftly away in the direction taken by the Plain Cree. He was tall and well-formed, and his features were regular—almost handsome, though delicate, under the thick coating of scarlet and yellow paint. Immediately after One Hand himself came around among his people. He entered each lodge and said quietly to the inmates:

"Keep inside and have your guns ready. The young man is gone to the fort. He will bring the mare if he has to shoot *Ohskatask*. If he kills him he will return fast, and when he enters the camp he will cry '*Nipahow!*' It will be the war-cry. Rush from your tents and drive straight at the lodges of the Plain Crees. Shoot them as they run out; crowd them into the river!"

Jim Vue sat in one of the tents, hugging a rifle loaned by an old Wood Indian. Beside him knelt the clerk with another gun, borrowed from a friendly halfbreed who had two. Bellwood's knees were shaking. Jim pulled at a cigarette and but for a slight smile and the sparkle of his black eyes, he appeared as usual.

"Blamed if this don't look pretty good!" he observed pleasantly to Bellwood. "It's the first time I've felt to home since I hit this doggoned camp. I'd like to see the curtain raise, though, I'm scared the thing'll fall through yet—I'm 'fraid it'll fall through. Hanged if my cigarette ain't went out, talkin' like a Chinaman; got a light? Thanks. I wouldn't mind startin' it myself, but then, y'u can't never depend on an Injun. Don't the *Kitche Musinagun* say: 'Put not your trust in Injuns?' 'Princes,' is it? Well, it's some time since I've went to Sunday school. Now, if it had been princesses, y'u might hev wrote me down a Agnes——? 'tic;' yes, 'Agnes' 's shorter; it's a good name, an' she's all right. I know a princess—but that's neither here nor there; at least, she's there, not here.

"Well, say I popped the first gun. Like as not them Wood Injuns'd all funk, an' how'd that look for me?—whole darned Plain Cree outfit to fight alone? Same's I heard ol' Judge Gumpus over to Boise, oncet, when the two opposin' 'torneys got to scrappin' in court. 'Gentlemen,' says he, quite polite, 'the Ter-ri-to-ry ain't payin' you for prosecutin' each other or defendin' yourselves. You're losin' your time.' That's what I'd be doin', losin' my time,—prosecutin' or defendin'.'"

"You might count on me for one, Jim," chattered Bellwood, "but don't do it. We can't afford to take such risks. Hang this waiting, anyhow! Once in the whirl, I'd be all right, but I'm all of a sh——"

A rattle of approaching hoofs interrupted. Jim and Bellwood peered eagerly out through holes in the deerskin lodge. One Hand's young man was coming at a racing gallop, and behind, at the end of her line, pounded the roan mare.

Not an Indian was to be seen about the camp. The Plain Crees must have been suspicious. The silence was pregnant. Bellwood's heart thumped slow and labouriously as he watched the lips of the young warrior coming, with the awful issues of life and death, like an oracle, behind them. But they were tightly sealed, and his face was immobile; it betrayed nothing. Onward he swung, straight in and to the centre of the camp. Suddenly the lips parted wide——

"*Nipahow!*"

"I have killed him!" It was the battle cry. A wave of naked, painted bodies rolled from the smoke-browned tepees and, with a mighty surge of sound from three hundred thewy throats, swept at the lodges of the Plain Crees. Instantly Stalking Spirit and his men appeared. A roar—a cloud of smoke, and a score fell at the doors of their tents. But the Plain Crees soon recovered. They had not been brought up fighting for nothing. They were not to be beaten in a minute. At their answering volley, Chief One Hand and five of his best men dropped. Terror fell upon the Wood Crees; they wavered. Immediately the wild, high voice of Stalking Spirit could be heard above the din, calling his war-cry, — "*Eyah-haw-hoy!—Eyah-haw-hoy!*"

" 'See nothing, say nothing; saw wood with a hammer'," quoted Jim Vue, imperturbably, eying the scene. "There's only two ways for this thing to go," he commented in a confidential tone to Bellwood. "One means sure death to us; perhaps the other does, too, but it's our only show. See these fellers—plumb whipped already because they've lost their chief. Stalking Spirit an' his six hoss team o' Plain Injuns 'll eat 'em up in a minute if they don't get somebody to lead 'em. Perhaps they won't fight anyway!"

Suddenly he tossed his hat in the air and burst into a long, ringing laugh that seemed something devilish, while the bullets of the now offensive Plain band whistled past him.

"Hurrah!" he shouted. "Chief for an hour! Hurrah! '*Nipahow!*' "

The dismayed Wood Crees looked at him in amazement. Had this white prisoner gone crazy? They forgot to be frightened, forgot to run away. The Plain Crees, too, paused, astonished. Stalking Spirit, murderer, most superstitious of men, trembled with a scared, yellow face. It was an ill omen, this crazy man. He had never seen anything just like this. He had fought the Blackfoot many times, but they were never led by a madman.

"*Weetigoos!*" he muttered, as an incantation against the wicked spell.

"*Nipahow!*" yelled Jim Vue again; and, again laughing loudly, he rushed full at Stalking Spirit, with a drawn knife playing in the sunlight above his black, glossy hair.

The war chief turned and—fled!

And now the Wood Crees took heart. They laughed, too, with this madman, and followed close to his heels. They could not get near enough to him. What a good joke it was, this man fighting for them, from whom the Plain Crees sped as from a pestilence! All they had to do was to chase them. And chase them they did, with a will. Over the brow of the bank, where the river curved far below, they flew; and the Wood Crees followed, always pressing round their dear madman. The squaws, too, fled with their little ones to rejoin their lords when they had recovered somewhat from the baleful magic.

But if Jim was a madman, he at least knew how to shoot. The war chief was flying over the rise of a knoll, half-way down the bank. Jim dropped on a knee—a puff of smoke and Stalking Spirit lay sprawled upon the knoll.

The Plain Crees were routed utterly and the Wood Indians, headed by Jim Vue and Bellwood, with triumphal songs returned to camp amid great rejoicing.

Soft Hair bent over her dead father, weeping silently.

"Poor old beggar!" said Jim, sympathetically:

'There was no one like 'im, 'Oss or Foot,
   Or any o' the Guns I knew;
An' because it was so, why, o'course 'e went an' died,
   W'ich is just what the best men do.'

"Where's '*Nipahow*,' I wonder?"

Soft Hair looked up as he spoke. She understood. Vermilion and yellow ochre covered her face, except where the tears had made little courses down it, through which showed her smooth, tawny skin.

"It was me that killed *Ohskatask*," she said, simply. "I did it for you."

Jim shot a delighted glance at her—alas! for *Minnishooshay*.

"Well, now! Ain't she a Jo-dandy! Ain't she a Jim-beaut!" he exclaimed with effusive admiration. Then he leaned over, caught her hand, and touched it with his lips; and when in time he left the Cree camp, Soft Hair went with him.

Thus it came about that when the troops under General Odds at length arrived at Fort Marais there were no Indians to engage, for Jim Vue and Bellwood and the old man led the Wood Crees into the general's camp under a flag of truce. Best of all, they brought with them the arch-rebel, the man who had begun the massacre at Singing Lake and had, with his own hand, slain two of the white men, the man the Government wanted above all others—Stalking Spirit, who had recovered from the wound given him by Jim. The night of the surrender, he made an abortive attempt to kill himself. He stuck a knife between his ribs, just missing the heart and cutting a lobe of lung so that a piece protruded. The surgeon put it back and once more he recovered—to die, five months later, ingloriously upon the scaffold.

V
THE INDIAN

By 1881 events had closed in on the Indians of the North-West. The free roaming days on the prairies had ended and the reserve reluctantly taken up. But there were still tales of early day adventures to be told—a fast-fading picture which those like Cameron could understand and capture for all time.

One of the first to write of Indians as individuals and personalities, he did not see them as a pack of stone-faced savages often portrayed in the literature of the times. Instead, the red man's humour was sometimes revealed in his dealings with pompous white officials, as Cameron relates. The author also preserved stories of violence and used his own experiences as a trader to create a realistic description of Indian life and customs in the late 1880s.

The Making of a Warrior
(Fiction)

Peace between the Crows and the Peigans had endured for longer
than *Absaroka* could remember, though that was because *Absaroka*
was a young man and had yet to win a warrior's plumes. *Tiparo,* head
chief of the Crows, who was *Absaroka's* father, could quite easily
recall a day when peace had not been between the tribes. He had
good cause to remember. His war plait was missing and, where it
used to grow on his crown was a bald spot which had not come
slowly and of its own volition, but suddenly and with a jerk.

But if the old chief had not forgotten, while a heathen he yet
possessed one, at least, of the Christian virtues; he had forgiven.
And here was *Matoxi* with his crowd of Peigan young men come
to visit him and their friends the Crows, as they had done often
before, and *Tiparo* said *"How!"* and shook their hands.

"My brother," said *Matoxi* to the Crow chief, as they sat that
night side by side at the dog feast and watched their young men
dance together. "You are old and have seen much, while I am but
a child at your feet." *Matoxi* was no child, but a full-grown man
and a warrior with a record of many scalps. It would have been ill
for another to have said this to him, but it was his present whim to
speak thus. "Tell me; I seek your counsel: These soldiers of the
Long Knives—can they fight?"

The Crow chief put out his hand in protest and looked toward
the ground. "It is not for me to say," he replied, gravely. "We have
no quarrel with the whites."

"But we! It is long since we fought the Crees, who are cowardly
whelps and love not battle, but to steal our horses. Our young
men chafe at idleness; they say soon there will be no more
warriors. They would fight the whites.

Reprinted from Field and Stream, *New York, April 1898.*

The old chief was silent for a moment. "The white men are not like your Crees," he said at length. "They are no cowards, though the Cutthroats [Sioux] put them out, as water drowns fire, at the Little Big Horn. Also, we are the servants of the Long Knives and fight with them. Your young men will do wisely to find other foes."

Matoxi looked very humble, but there was a sharp twinkle in his dark eyes and a suggestion of menace in his tone as he replied:

"The young men chafe. They will not look far—nor long—for an enemy. But," he added, grasping the hand of the older man warmly and bending toward him, "between you and me, my brother, and between our peoples, may there be always peace."

"See!" exclaimed *Tiparo*. "My son spears the white dog's head. I stake my tongue he does it well for the entertainment of the Peigan chief whose name is loud in the land."

Absaroka knelt within the encircling rows of the Crows and the Peigans with his body thrown forward and his hands resting on the ground. The palms were outspread on the hard, smooth earth. Across his forehead from his scalplock fell an eagle plume. Broad bands of brass circled his wrists and ankles and strips of otter his elbows and knees. A string of bells crossed his chest. His legs and arms were streaked with ochre and white mud. His eyes were the centres of stars, from which black points radiated. Across his cheek slanted three scarlet bars and his chin was marked with alternate bands of blue and yellow. A narrow breechcloth was wound loosely about his hips and thighs. Moccasins gaily beaded covered his feet. The glossy, royal skin of a silver fox was fixed lightly over his shoulder; the splendid tail hung far down his back. Planted in the ground before him was his spear, decked with ribbons and feathers; and farther on, in the centre of the circle, stood the great kettle which held the white dog's head.

The painted war drum hung a few inches from the ground, upheld on four pointed willow withes. Around it sat the six drummers. The first drummer struck the drum a light tap with his stick, and taking the highest note in his compass, the war song had begun.

The voices of the other drummers swelled the weird, strange chant, and to the rhythmic beat of the drum, it gradually fell, fell, until the lowest strain, a deep bass, was reached, and dwelt upon. Thence it jumped abruptly to the beginning, and again it fell, gradually, to the bass—and again to the beginning, to be repeated—and again.

At the first tap of the drum, the tall, lithe figure of *Absaroka* began to sway, back and forth and from side to side, in time with the chant, and his hands to brush lightly the damp, bare soil. He raised them and rubbed them softly together; then dropped and moved them over the earth again. Suddenly he sprang to his feet, catching up his spear, and commenced to dance. His eyes flashed. The thews and muscles of his limbs and chest stood out like great ropes, or rolled and rippled under the smooth, copper skin like the coils of an immense snake. He circled about the white dog's head as though it were an enemy, ready to strike should he approach too near; then darted away, uttering a shrill war cry, crouching along the ground, all the while keeping step to the measured *pom! pom! pom! pom!* of the big drum and the wild, plaintive chant of the drummers. His body leaned and stayed, pitched and glided, as he drew nearer and nearer to the kettle, with all the grace and agility of the puma stealing upon its prey. The jet-tipped eagle plume in his plaited hair nodded back and forth with the movements of his body. His eyes glowed fiercely in the reflection of the fire. His face was set and drawn.

He crept nearer to the kettle. He lifted his spear, and with a quick bound launched it at the head of the white dog. The drum stopped. He drew himself up, placed his fingers over his lips and gave a long, piercing, staccato yell. It was the *coup*—the death. He raised the kettle and carried it three times around in a circle. Perspiration streamed from him as he walked over and took his seat. A roar of applause came from the warriors and a volley sounded from the big drum.

"Your tongue is a single one," said *Matoxi* to *Tiparo*. "He is a great dancer. He will make a warrior."

Tiparo smiled proudly. "Come, my brother," he said, as a pan of the steaming flesh was set before them. "Eat. The white dog is warriors' meat."

At the close of the feast the warriors danced with short, jerky steps in solemn procession around the circle. Then with the mystic word "*Weetigoos!*" muttered by each in turn as a shield against the power of the cannibal devil, they passed one by one out of the shadow of the flickering firelight, and so to their lodges and to sleep.

The sun almost topped the yellow hills looking down upon the emerald ribbon of the Bowstring and the Crow camp before *Absaroka* stirred in his blanket and stretched his protesting limbs, stiff from the heavy strain he had put upon them the night before. He opened his eyes and called to his wife, *Wapah*, to prepare breakfast. He lifted the flap of his lodge door and stepped out.

The valley was bathed in blue and purple; the hills above were golden with the gold of midsummer. Save for the murmur of the rapid above the camp and the gnawing of a wolfish-looking cur on a bone in the grass before him, not a sound profaned the solemn stillness of the morning. He raised his arms high above his head, breathing deep of the fresh, sweet air; picked up a stone and threw it at the dog, which shambled off, snarling, with its tail between its legs.

Absaroka stood for a moment drinking in the profound tranquility, the unsullied loveliness of this new day. He gave a gasp of keen delight and his eyes sparkled with reawakened vigour.

"Ah! it is good to be alive," he said, softly, to himself.

Then he turned and walked over to his father's lodge to pay his early respects to *Tiparo's* visitor.

The light was still dim within but he could see that it was occupied by but one reclining figure. He entered quickly and stooping, raised the blanket which covered the face of the sleeper. He started back with a smothered exclamation and with widely-staring eyes burst from the lodge.

"*Wanaska! Wanaska!* Awake! Awake!" he cried. "Your chief is dead — dead by the knife of *Matoxi! Eyaw-haw-hoy!*" And he gave the Crow war whoop.

They came tumbling out of their lodges, stunned and doubting.

"It is the truth!" he cried again. "The Peigan dogs have also taken our horses,—all but mine, which I hid after nightfall. Follow, twenty of you. We will take them and pick up the trail of these false friends who strike in the dark. We will ride them into the ground!"

The Crow war cry rang loud and fiercely through the camp. *Absaroka* caught up a line and ran down along the river to a bend where he sprang into the water and swam rapidly to an island in the middle. Pushing through the willow thickets, he came to an open space in the centre where a band of magnificent horses was grazing. Singling out the finest, a splendid bay, he whirled his hair lariat in the air and it flew true to the mark as the animal plunged to escape it. The loop passed over the horse's ears and tightened around his windpipe. *Absaroka* leaped upon his back and drove the others before him to the camp.

The Crows were already attired for the war path; stripped, painted and feathered, armed with bows, quivers, spears and buffalo hide shields, and carrying food enough only for their morning meal as they rode—a little dried meat. There were just twenty of them in all. Once they rode slowly around the camp, chanting their war song. Then together they beat their heels against the ribs of their horses and disappeared over the hills above the camp in a small cloud of yellow dust.

It was not until the second night that they warily neared the Peigan war party. They lay through the darkness in a fringe of willows along a sickly stream that wandered across the face of the wide, bare plain, watching the camp fires of the enemy. The horses which the Peigans had taken were many and good. They did not know that *Absaroka* still had the best of them, or they should have been less careless. They had ridden hard; on the following day they should reach their people and they felt no sense of danger or fear of surprise. They slept the sleep of weariness and security.

There were forty of the Peigans and as the gray dawn began to filter through the night, they sprang from the ground with the Crow battle cry ringing in their ears. As they did so, arrows rained upon them from the attacking party and many fell where they stood. Some of the tethered horses broke away and ran madly across the plain. The unwounded Peigans jumped upon the backs of others and fled, demoralized, before the onslaught of the vengeful Crows.

And now began a chase that was stern and long, a battle on horseback. For hours it kept up, with unwearying, deadly persistence on the part of the Crows and growing dread and hopelessness on the side of the Peigans. One by one the saddles of the pursued were emptied and their riderless and winded horses stepped aside out of the bloody course and dropped behind. The Peigans were now fewer in number, though four of the Crows had also fallen.

The sure shafts of *Absaroka* had pierced three of the enemy, his spear another. Yet he was not satisfied. They had been men who came between him and his prey; he had eyes only for one man, *Matoxi*, who rode his own horse—a white he had brought with him on this visit, almost the match of *Absaroka's* bay—and kept at the head of the long race.

But now *Absaroka* pressed him hard; an arrow from his bow caught the Peigan's horse in the neck and he stumbled and rolled over, throwing *Matoxi* to the earth. Instantly he was upon his feet and threw his shield before his face. *Absaroka's* horse had carried him beyond the Peigan, but he wheeled about.

"This for you, *Matoxi!*" he called as he swung past again, with his bow drawn to the full reach of his arm.

The bowstring twanged and *Matoxi* sank to the ground with the heavy bullhide shield fixed on his breast.

Absaroka rode on. Several of the Peigans were in the lead again. One leaping from his own jaded pony to the saddle of a horse emptied by a dying Crow, outstripped the others. *Absaroka* rode close behind another with his spear aloft.

The man cringed upon the neck of his steed. *Absaroka* lunged and the blade passed through the Peigan's neck. *Absaroka* pulled in his blowing horse and laughed.

"I did not expect to spear the dog's head so soon again," he said.

He had reached the head of the fighting line. There were no mounted enemies behind him. Far ahead, the solitary Peigan rode on, doggedly; desperately, with his precious life. *Absaroka* signalled to his men to stop.

"It is enough!" he cried. "Let him go. Let him return to his people and tell them what the Crows did to the Peigans!"

He turned and galloped hard back to where the Peigan chief lay, breathing painfully. He dismounted and walked towards him, the Peigan watching as he approached.

"You wear a medal on your breast, like an English officer," said *Absaroka* in a mocking voice, pointing to the shield. "But it is bigger. And you have no right to wear the mark of a soldier; you are no brave."

He stooped and snatched the shield and arrow roughly from *Matoxi's* breast. The blood spurted forth. The Peigan writhed.

"Painted Cheek dog!" hissed *Absaroka* and he stepped nearer, drawing his knife.

On either side the yellow plain swept away limitless; the solitary Peigan was a speck on the horizon. The sun rode majestically through the spotless blue sky.

The yellow ochre upon the face of *Matoxi* did not betray the ghastly pallor of the skin beneath. He smiled up at the young Crow.

"I spoke truly," he said, faintly. "I told your father the night you speared the white dog's head as I never saw it done before, that you would make a warrior."

Costumes of the Plains Indians

Look at a coloured print of an American Indian as customarily displayed for sale in drug or tobacco stores and what do you see? A face, often handsome, intelligent, with skin of a copper tint, set in a gorgeous frame of black-tipped eagle tail plumes. The Indian whose person is dominated by this finely featured face is probably wearing a fringed buckskin coat or shirt, decorated by small artistically beaded rosettes from which depend scalps, tufts of dyed horsehair or coloured ribbon, beaded blue or scarlet stroud leggings and moccasins, the uppers worked in novel geometric designs with coloured beads. And usually he is carrying a rifle. Altogether our red brother is a striking and picturesque figure.

From these showy and eye-filling trappings the average white man is likely to get an erroneous conception of the Indian's customary dress and think that the red man was always arrayed in such habiliments, even when on the warpath or in battle. This is a misconception which calls for deflating. The showy apparel was the red man's "top hat, white tie and tails"; he wore it only on special occasions—when on parade, at ceremonial dances, receptions of tribal or paleface dignitaries, or other state affairs. Customarily there was nothing very spectacular or attractive about the garb of the ordinary Indian. His usual dress was of the decidedly nondescript pattern.

There were exceptions—dandies among them. Little Poplar for example. I first saw him in the spring of 1884. He had recently come from across "the Line"—Montana—with several of his six wives, one a Crow woman, and he was quite elaborately attired. Starting at the top, he wore a broad-brimmed Stetson hat with a

Reprinted from The Beaver, *Winnipeg, Man., September 1943.*

flexible brass band, an eagle feather stuck in the side, a fancy blanket over his left shoulder supported at the waist by a broad brass-studded leather belt from which hung in a thick leather scabbard one of the heavy broad-bladed "buffalo" knives sold by the Hudson's Bay Company, and a 45 calibre Colt six shooter. Heavily beaded cloth leggings and moccasins completed his dress and of course he carried a rifle. He was insolently berating Farming Instructor Delaney (one of the victims the next year of the Frog Lake Massacre) for his supposed niggardliness in handing out rations—meaning provisions—to the Indians, though the instructor of course could ration them only to the extent that he had authority. Little Poplar was one of the band's councillors. His brother, Nacotan, another of Chief Big Bear's followers, also showed his weakness for finery and often appeared "dressed up."

In May of the following spring I again saw Little Poplar—I believe for the last time. I was then a prisoner of Big Bear's band and we were camped in the valley of the Little Red Deer River when word of the arrival at Fort Pitt of the *chemoginusuk* (the soldiers) reached us. In the early morning of the 28th, Little Poplar rode through the camp quavering the Cree war song and upbraiding some of his laggard or timid fellow tribesmen for their tardiness in preparing to fight. From somewhere or other he had dug up a small bowler hat and this, with a brass-studded vest, a breechclout and moccasins, completed his wardrobe. His legs and the rest of his body were bare, but streaked with white mud. Across his pony's withers lay his Winchester rifle. Nothing gaudy about Little Poplar this May morning of 1885.

By way of contrast, let's take a look at the old chief, Big Bear. I am not sure when I first saw him, but I recall vividly a day in 1884 in old Battleford when a large party of Plains Cree, headed by the two principal chiefs, came into the old territorial capital on a hunger or "begging" dance. These were quite in the character of events. The Indians, barring paint and feathers, were for the most part naked. Big Bear on this occasion was garbed in an ordinary black suit which had once been new, a soft black felt hat and unadorned moccasins. Seated on the ground before Sandy Macdonald's store in the old town, the Indians formed a circle and Big Bear, mounted on a white horse, rode up and down in front of it, proclaiming in a loud voice: *"Tapway, meewasin omah, Nootendo Seepee! Tapway namoya iyumun omah!"* (Certainly, it is good here, Battle River [the Cree name for Battleford]. Of a certainty it is not hard—difficult—here!) He meant that it was a good place—that they were being well treated, when the trader piled up flour and other provisions and tobacco before the dancers in payment for the entertainment.

I cannot recall ever seeing Big Bear painted or wearing any finery, even on special occasions. His usual attire was a rough shirt, a blanket and moccasins. Unlike Poundmaker, whose hair (of which he was inordinately proud) fell in two enormous shining black plaits to his knees, Big Bear's locks, to which apparently he gave little thought, were rather short and unkempt.

Poundmaker was an extremely handsome and dignified Indian, with the features of a Roman senator, and undoubtedly was quite conscious of it. At the Battleford begging dance he wore on his head the dried skin of a bird, a vest studded with brass nails, bangles on his arms, and moccasins, his bare legs streaked with white paint. But his everyday attire was a belted white Hudson's Bay blanket, cloth leggings and moccasins. Nothing gaudy about Chief Poundmaker on his occasional visits to Battleford from the reserve thirty miles away; his natural dignity, however, needed no artificial embellishments to enhance it.

Imasees, Big Bear's second son, the instigator of the Frog Lake Massacre, on the other hand, liked to "dress up." Having a high opinion of himself, and being naturally a truculent young ruffian, he usually was painted and wore some finery. He paid particular attention to his hair, which was worn in braided plaits bound with beaded and metal bands. He was beribboned and bedecked from head to foot on ceremonial occasions and was never without some modicum of ornamental attire.

Imasees as a young brave was one of the finest specimens of physical manhood I have ever seen. He was not tall—five feet eight or nine perhaps—but he possessed a figure that was the perfect embodiment of grace and strength—a form that, stripped, was a delight to look upon. Despite his treacherous and bloodthirsty character, I could not help entertaining for him a measure of secret admiration. His father, Big Bear, when young must have possessed a somewhat similar figure, though it never, I am certain, housed such an evil and sinister spirit as did that of his formidable son.

In a group photograph of Indians, Mounted Police and Hudson's Bay officials taken in 1884 at Fort Pitt on the North Saskatchewan, the Indians including Big Bear, his son King Bird, and Four Sky Thunder, a councillor, are shown wearing fancy blankets and stiff felt hats, decorated with bands of ribbon and bunched feather uprights. This, however, was a posed picture and these trappings were Hudson's Bay Company property loaned for the occasion. These bunched feathers were coloured, chiefly red and blue, and imported by the Company for the Indian trade. They were from stock no longer fashionable in civilization but were looked upon by the red men as highly desirable embellishments and their fortunate possessors were regarded by their fellow tribesmen with envy and respect as wealthy and exalted individuals.

The large elaborate feathered headdresses which have become so familiar to the general public in recent years were not common among the Plains Crees in an earlier era. They are really more show pieces than anything else and made chiefly for sale to wealthy white visitors to the West who are willing to pay the comparatively high prices demanded. In short they have become an article of commerce and source of revenue to the astute red man, and therefore no longer have the significance that once attached to them, marking the wearer as a personage of distinction, such as a chief or warrior. They originated among the Sioux and other warlike tribes south of the 49th parallel and in time came into use in the Canadian West as a result of raids or visits by Canadian Indians in the territories of their American neighbours.

When the Assiniboines—or Stoneys, as they are commonly called—an offshoot of the Sioux, came into Battleford on a begging dance, they gave the inhabitants of that rambling collection of shacks on the banks of the Battle River a true primeval thrill. Gorgeous in paint and feathers, carrying their war drum, coup sticks and rifles, they formed up abreast at the upper end of Battleford's one street and advanced, chanting their war song, crowing and dancing, to the accompaniment of the booming drum the whole length of the town, halting by the way at the three different trading posts—Frank Smart's, Mahoney and Macdonald's and the Hudson's Bay Company's—to dance, orate and "count coups" in the striking and resounding Assiniboine-Sioux speech. Payment having been made by the trader in flour, bacon, tea, sugar and tobacco for the honour being ostensibly accorded him, they moved on to the next "port of call" to repeat their performance. At intervals they punctuated their thrilling act by volleys from their guns. Altogether, a visit from the Stoneys counted as a field day in the rather humdrum life of the old North-West capital.

The Stoneys were a picturesque lot and more given, perhaps, than were the Crees to sartorial adornment, though their garb was also drab and scanty enough as a general thing. They all wore the blanket, which was the almost universal everyday wrap of both the Plains and the Woods Indians. In fact as a rule they wore little else except breechclout and moccasins, though in cold weather they usually added cloth leggings, mittens and a sash or belt.

In talking years ago with Charlie Russell, the famous cowboy artist of Montana, he told me how Tom Mix had wanted him to go up to the buffalo park at Wainwright, Alberta, with a party of Indians, to direct them in a picture. The park had become overpopulated; it contained more animals than it would supply food for, and the Dominion government had decided to reduce the herd by killing off a considerable number and selling the meat and robes. Mix had obtained permission to do the slaughtering and planned to make a spectacle of it by having the Indians "run" the buffalo in a revival of the oldtime buffalo hunt. Russell declined on some pretext or other.

"I didn't want any part of it," he told me afterwards. "I knew Mix's idea would be to make a holy show of it—something 'colossal'; have his Indians all paint and feathers from moccasin sole to scalplock in the approved motion picture style. Indians fought or ran buffalo naked unless you reckon moccasins and a breechclout a full suit of clothes. I didn't want the public to get the idea that I knew so little about Indians as to be responsible for staging such a phoney exhibition."

In my experience, the article most prized in the 1880s by a Plains Cree was an otter skin, a whole unslit pelt in the form of a cuff topping the plaits of his coal-black hair. In skinning, a pelt was turned, or "cased" much as one turns a sock, the full length of the carcass from tail to nose, which left the detached skin flesh side out. After fleshing and dressing, the pelt was again turned, when it was in the same form as when worn by the animal—that is, with the rich glossy fur exposed. Lynx skins, prepared in similar fashion, were popular, and being much more plentiful and far less valuable than otter, were in more general use.

The common dress of Indian women was a sleeveless cotton blouse or shirt, a short skirt of the same material, leggings, moccasins and a blanket or tartan shawl. However, I remember seeing one at a ball at the Mounted Police barracks at Battleford robed in white muslin and a young woman at another dance in the same town wearing a pink calico dress. And in both instances the thermometer outside callously recorded a temperature of 40 below! The Indian woman carefully brushed, oiled and plaited her hair, and in the middle where the part came there was usually a streak of gay vermilion, with which cheerful aid to beauty she frequently brightened her often smooth and quite attractive features.

Now, as a final word, let me give some idea of the usual dress of

that remarkable Indian and war chief or head soldier—
Kahpaypamahchakwayo, or Wandering Spirit.

First, his cap, which was the lynx skin cuff before described,
from which dangled five jet-tipped eagle-tail plumes. (For each of
these, as he was fond of proclaiming, he meant to have a white
man's scalp.) He wore a green and white blanket coat, belted at
the middle, cloth leggings, breechclout and moccasins. His black
hair was wavy, almost curly—an odd thing in an Indian—and
wreathed his cruel face, with its thin lips and piercing sultry eyes,
like a sombre halo. Excited or provoked, his sultry eyes took on a
darker and even deadlier shade; one almost expected to see them
throw off fire as sparks fly from a smitten stone. He symbolized
the tiger in human form.

But now look again at Wandering Spirit. It is the morning that
word reaches us in the Indian camp in the Little Red Deer valley
that the ground about burned and abandoned Fort Pitt, twenty
miles to the west, is white with the tents of the *chemoginusuk*—the
troops of the Alberta Field Force under General Strange. Stripped
to the skin, wearing breechclout and moccasins only, Winchester
in hand and bands of cartridges encircling his body, astride his tall
gray mare, his eyes flashing and black hair tossing in the wind, he
makes the round of the two hundred lodges, the long ringing Cree
war cry bursting from his lips, calling on his followers to prepare
for battle. He has cast aside any tawdry ornament or garment
which will impede or cramp his movements so that he may slip
presently like a snake through the grass or brush, his hot heart
burning with the lust to kill. He has taken thirteen Blackfoot
scalps. He is the living, breathing illustration of a vanished
type—the Indian warrior on the warpath.

The Last of the Snakes

Look at a map of the region now within the boundaries of Jasper National Park, in the province of Alberta, and you will see (if your map is a good one) some distance to the north and west of the present town of Jasper a stream marked "Snake Indian River." But if you are interested in Indians and ask where members of this particular tribe are to be found you will not be told, because there are no longer any Snake Indians. And if it were not that a hint of their one-time existence endures in the name of this stream, doubtless the knowledge that there ever was such a tribe would long since have been lost. The manner and cause of their disappearance is the matter of this story.

About the year 1842—the exact date is difficult to fix—the Snakes, a small tribe consisting of some twenty families, were invited by their enemies the Assiniboines—a much more numerous and aggressive tribe—to a grand council at their main village on Lac Brule for the purpose of arranging a treaty of peace. It was stipulated that both parties to the negotiations come unarmed.

Accepting the advances of their enemies in good faith, the Snakes came in a body, leaving their arms at home.

The treachery of the Assiniboines was soon to appear, however, for the peace talk had not gone far into the night when at a prearranged signal they suddenly drew guns hidden beneath their blankets and cold-bloodedly shot to death every Snake present with the exception of three young women. These they bound and placed in an unoccupied lodge with the intention of sacrificing them at the scalp dance to be held next day. Meanwhile a few

Manuscript in the Cameron Papers. Another version of the story appeared in When Fur Was King, *by H. J. Moberly and W. B. Cameron. (Toronto: J. M. Dent and Sons Ltd., 1929).*

young men were dispatched to the Snake Indian village to dispose of those whom old age or illness had prevented from attending the council.

A French halfbreed in the camp named Bellerose, shocked by the outrage and pitying the helpless survivors, stole into their lodge during the night and cut their bonds. "Here is my big skinning knife and my firebag containing flint and steel," he told them in a whisper. "Also a little dried meat. I can give you nothing more. Now, start as soon as you can and keep going. Make no noise. Get into the water along shore so that you will leave no tracks. When day comes, go into the thick woods—be careful not to walk on damp ground—and hide until night comes again. If they do not find you for two days they will likely give up looking for you and you will be safe."

The young women did as they had been instructed, they saw none of their enemies and at length they reached the mouth of the Baptiste River, now shown on the map as the Berland, which flows into the Athabasca from the west. They could not agree on their further course and so at this point they parted. Two were determined to keep on down the Athabasca. They made a raft, crossed the Baptiste and taking with them the firebag, flint and steel, continued to follow the larger stream. They were never afterward heard of and were probably either drowned or overtaken by the Assiniboines and killed.

The third girl, believing it would be safest, now left with only the knife, turned up the Berland and after travelling for several days reached a wooded valley deep in the mountains, where she decided to winter and set about making her preparations. Berries were plentiful and she gathered and dried a considerable supply. She managed to kill a few squirrels with stones and from the sinews in their tails fashioned snares for rabbits, which were also numerous. She killed some porcupines and dried the meat and out of rabbit skins made herself a warm winter coat, sewn together with sinew. She kindled a fire in the primitive way by revolving the point of one dry stick in a hole made in another and collected a large pile of dry wood. And so by the time winter set in she was prepared for it.

The following summer an Iroquois hunter, wandering far from his usual haunts, was startled to come upon a series of strange tracks and marks. He wondered. What animal or creature could have left such mysterious traces? A *weetigo*, perhaps—that evil being in the form of a man that devoured people?

He shuddered. With frequent glances over his shoulder, he hurried away from the locality.

But the next summer, when the Iroquois were in camp a short distance from the Berland, the hunter, taking his courage in his hands, determined he would learn definitely what it was had made the sinister tracks. He struck the river where the Snake woman was now living (she had moved in the meantime), saw snares set, trees barked and fresh footprints resembling those of a human being. He was a plucky man and certain now that he had come upon a real *weetigo*, determined to hunt and kill him.

Creeping cautiously round, with his gun at full cock and expecting at any moment to be pounced upon, he came to a high bank at the foot of which he saw a great pile of dry wood, with a fire burning beside it, close to the entrance of a small cave. There was no other sign of life.

He hid himself close to the cave and presently a strange creature in a short fuzzy skirt, carrying a load of rabbits, came in sight. Throwing down the pack, this grotesque object picked up some sticks with which to feed the fire. Recognizing the sex the hunter knew at once that she must be one of the three young women who two years before had escaped the massacre of the Snake Indians at Lac Brule.

Happening to look up, the woman saw him. She turned instantly and ran in a frantic effort to escape, but was soon overtaken. She had become quite wild and he was forced to handle her like an untamed animal in order to get her to his camp, where she again became a normal human being. She remained with his family for two years. Then the Hudson's Bay Company officer at Jasper House employed her for another two years as a servant at the trading post, at the end of which time she married a Shuswap Indian.

She was the last of the Snakes.

Almighty Voice

Kisse-manito-wayo, or Almighty Voice, was a red man of spirit. He belonged to One Arrow's band of Crees, whose reserve lies a little to the eastward of Batoche on the South Saskatchewan River. Almighty Voice had an ambition, born or acquired, to be great. Many young Indians yearn to soar, but at this day seldom has one the courage to sprout wings. Almighty Voice had. That was where he showed himself, in a manner, superior to most other young Indians.

In the abstract, there is nothing reprehensible about a longing for distinction. Unfortunately, however, ideals of the red and white races differ; and the North American savage has yet to be persuaded that the noblest pursuit a man can engage in is not the pursuit of many wives, untended stock and scalps.

The ambition of Almighty Voice was kept carefully in the background until he had seen, perhaps, eighteen summers. Louis Marion, who had instructed the boy's father, Sounding Sky, in the wonders of agriculture, had known him since his black little head reached barely to the big instructor's knee and had never noted anything especially unpromising in the boy's character. He was wilful, it is true, and when ordered to go with the others to the swamps at the hay making or to tend his father's cattle when Sounding Sky was absent on a brief hunt, he sometimes smiled inscrutably out of his deep black eyes—and then taking a gun, went hunting on his own account. Most of the young bucks were wilful, however, and occasionally Almighty Voice responded cheerfully enough to the authority of government in the person of his farming instructor.

But no sooner had Almighty Voice passed out of boyhood and

Reprinted from Scarlet and Gold Annual, *Vancouver, B.C., 1920.*

begun to think himself something of a man than he developed another inauspicious trait—inconstancy.

First he took *Napaise's* daughter, a girl thirteen years of age, to wife, after the Indian fashion. He was about sixteen. He kept her one summer; then he threw her away and married *Kapahoo's* girl. She was young, too, and he paid a small steer for her. He kept her also for a summer; but he could not recover the steer because the girl's mother, who was a shrewd old lady, had immediately made dried meat of him. She knew Almighty Voice.

After that he took The Rump's daughter. I was clerk at Duck Lake Indian agency a part of this time and saw Almighty Voice often. I remember well the trouble these matrimonial vagaries of his caused. The Indian agent remonstrated with him. He said the youth must take his first wife, wed her in correct form and for the future cleave to her alone.

"I won't live with that offal," was Almighty Voice's short response.

He was told that, at all events, he could have but one wife and that if he attempted to keep more he would be arrested and punished. Then Almighty Voice went into rebellion. He knew older men with six wives; why could he not have as many if he chose?

He still lived with his last wife, but he had lost his fickle heart to another dark-skinned beauty of his people. She was a girl from Fort à la Corne, a granddaughter of Old Dust, and Almighty Voice made ardent love to her. Soon after this his brother-in-law Larocque, son of *Napaise*, came to the instructor and laid information against Almighty Voice for killing a steer. No one ever knew to whom it had belonged; only that it had not been the property of Almighty Voice.

It was the season of annuity payments to the Indians; and when, on October 22, 1895, Almighty Voice came forward to get his money, he was promptly arrested by Sergt. Colebrooke of the Batoche detachment, North-West Mounted Police. He had not known anything about the information. He was taken to Duck Lake and lodged, with another young Indian implicated in the killing, in the Mounted Police barracks at that place. The name of his accomplice was Dublin, a son of The Rump and consequently Almighty Voice's brother-in-law, also. Proof would be difficult, and it was the intention of the magistrates to explain to the delinquents in the morning that Indians and other people were not permitted to kill cattle which did not belong to them, and then to let them go again. In the morning Almighty Voice could not be produced.

He had been wholly unfettered. During the night the policeman on guard stepped outside for a minute and when he returned Almighty Voice was not there. He had tried to persuade Dublin to accompany him, but the other declined.

The unprofitableness of cattle killing having been duly impressed upon Dublin, he was allowed to return to his reserve. Sergt. Colebrooke and others of the Mounted Police came to One Arrow's and searched for several days, but, although he was about, they did not find Almighty Voice. Then Colebrooke learned that he had left The Rump's daughter and started with his newest love in the direction of La Corne. Colebrooke took an Indian guide with him in his buckboard and followed.

Meanwhile, Joe MacKay, interpreter to the Mounted Police at Prince Albert, had been despatched on the same quest. Fort à la Corne lies some fifty miles to the northeast of One Arrow's reserve.

A light snow fell the night after Colebrooke started and soon they came upon the tracks of Almighty Voice and his pony. His girl was riding. Later, Colebrooke met MacKay. The trail kept well to the poplar bluffs and was difficult to follow with wheels, so Colebrooke sent the buckboard back to Prince Albert with MacKay. Colebrooke and the guide went on till evening. By this time the trail had become quite fresh. Then they camped.

In the morning they were early on the move. It was October 29th. The had not gone far when they heard a shot. They spurred over a hill and came upon Almighty Voice. He had just killed a prairie chicken and was re-charging his gun—a muzzleloader.

"Don't go close," whispered the guide. "He shoot."

Colebrooke did not heed the warning. He did what the Mounted Police had been accustomed to do in the face of menace—went forward. It was a tradition of "The Force" that that was the only method. It was the one they had followed ever since their arrival in the country in 1874—usually with success.

Almighty Voice had retreated, facing the sergeant. His gun was now loaded. He dropped upon one knee and leveled it on the policeman. There was a dangerous gleam in his eye.

"*Awustay, Chemoginus!*" he said, sullenly, in Cree. "Keep off, soldier! I will shoot you. I will kill you."

The sergeant kept on. He was speaking in low, persuasive tones to the Indian—asking him to surrender himself peaceably.

"Come back!" called the terrified guide. "Come away. He kill you!"

Almighty Voice arose and retreated a little farther. He dropped on his knee and repeated his warning. The sergeant gripped the revolver in his left overcoat pocket a little tighter and kept on. The Indian arose again and walked backward a few paces. There was a willow bluff behind him, now; it would be convenient to jump into for cover if he missed. The girl sat on the pony a short distance away. She was sobbing.

"*Kaweeah! Kaweeah!* Don't! Don't!" she cried to her lover.

He was on his knee again and his aim rested on the policeman.

"*Awustay, Chemoginus!* I will shoot you!"

The sergeant raised his right hand and pressed forward, continuing his persuasive talk. Then Almighty Voice's gun rang out, and Colebrooke rolled forward in the saddle and slipped to the ground with a bullet through his heart. As the guide turned to run Almighty Voice sprang into the bluff.

In the afternoon, when the guide returned with some of the Carrot River settlers and another policeman, he found the sergeant lying just as he had fallen. Nothing, not even his revolver, had been touched. But darkness soon closed in and they were unable to follow the trail of Almighty Voice far. Poor Colebrooke was taken home to his distracted wife, and buried.

A few days later the Indian girl came to the Hudson's Bay Company's post at La Corne to purchase provisions. She was arrested and taken to Prince Albert. Naturally, she could not in the least explain what had become of Almighty Voice.

That was the ending of the first chapter in the story of Almighty Voice's ambition.

A winter, a summer and another winter passed, but they brought no certain tidings of Almighty Voice. A reward of $500 was offered for his capture. Rumour was constantly busy. It was reported, first that he was here, then there and next in a different part of the country altogether. The police were hot on the heels of these reports. They combed the country up and down and across, and then combed it again. No reliable trace of Almighty Voice could they uncover. It was most exasperating.

Solomon Venne was a French halfbreed rancher on the old trail to Qu'Appelle, ten miles east of One Arrow's reserve. On Wednesday, May 26th, 1897, David and Napoleon Venne, his sons, noticed three mounted Indians chasing some of their cattle near a bluff to the eastward of the ranch. They went in pursuit of the Indians, who made for the bluff. The pony of one of them, however, caught his foot in a badger hole and fell, and the Indian was captured. He was a young Saulteaux, a cousin of Almighty Voice, and was unarmed. One of his companions, he said, was

Dublin; who the other was he would not divulge. The Vennes liberated him and Napoleon rode to the barracks at Batoche to report.

At last, it seemed, they were on the trail of Almighty Voice. No time was to be lost. One Arrow's band was in camp at the Lizard Hills, seven miles beyond Venne's ranch, digging seneca root to sell to the traders, Sounding Sky had his lodge a mile from the others.

Corporal Bowdridge passed the information on to Inspector Wilson at Duck Lake, then threw the saddle on his horse and left at once with Venne for Sounding Sky's lodge. If Almighty Voice were really in the vicinity, he was as likely to be found in his father's camp as anywhere.

They did not find him at Sounding Sky's lodge, however. The old man took the trouble to explain to Venne that association with the police might be attended with harmful results to himself, and they went on to the main Indian camp. Here they discovered that the young Saulteaux had purchased a gun from one of the Indians the night before. He had given his horse for it.

As Bowdridge stood near the lodges he noticed two Indians run into a bluff a quarter of a mile away. There was a small hill at either end of it. He said to Venne: "You go to the top of that hill on the right and I'll take the other. We'll see that they don't steal out, and when Wilson comes we'll get 'em."

Venne passed too close to the bluff. There was a shot; then another. The first shattered his shoulder, the second the butt of his rifle. He crawled out of range, had his wound bound up in flour to check the flow of blood; then an Indian drove him in a buckboard to his father's ranch, Bowdridge staying behind to wait for Wilson. A messenger was despatched to Duck Lake, twenty miles away, for Dr. Stewart, and there was a lull while red and white breathed hard and waited for what was coming next.

One Arrow's band grew frightened after Venne was shot and moved back to their reserve the same day—all but Sounding Sky. Dr. Stewart reached Venne's the same night and returned to Duck Lake with the wounded man and his father. Inspector Wilson telegraphed the news of the shooting to headquarters at Prince Albert on Thursday night and left on Friday morning with four men for the Lizard Hills, where he arrested Sounding Sky on the charge of threatening Venne. Then Wilson sat down to await the arrival of reinforcements from Prince Albert. He supposed Almighty Voice might still be in the vicinity.

In the meantime Captain Jack Allan of the Mounted Police had left Prince Albert with a detachment of eleven men for the Lizard

Hills. At half past 8 o'clock on Friday morning, as they came over the top of a ridge some three miles east of the boundary of One Arrow's reserve, they saw two dark objects disappear in a bluff below them. Some of the men said they were Indians; others deer. The Lizard Hills were fifteen miles away; it seemed improbable that it was Almighty Voice. Captain Allan and Sergt. Raven rode forward to investigate, the men following at a distance. They entered the edge of the bluff. If the objects were deer they would run out.

They were Indians, not deer, and they lost no time in letting the fact be known. Their opening fire brought Allan off his horse, on the skirt of the bluff, with a shattered arm. His men rushed in and bore him out. Raven got a glimpse of an Indian and shot him in the ankle with his revolver.

Captain Allan was sent back to Prince Albert. Then the fight went on, the Indians singing war songs in the intervals.

If you stand in the doorway of what was Louis Marion's house on One Arrow's reserve and look in a northeasterly direction six miles over the grass knolls and thicketed hollows stretching between, you will see the high *Minichinass* (The Outside Hill) of the Crees, and you will know that you are gazing over the top of Almighty Voice's bluff which nestles in the broad, open valley close under its foot. That is where Captain Allan found the Indians.

The skirmish went on spiritedly until Raven got a ball through the thigh. Then the command devolved upon Corporal Hockin. Hockin had been a captain in the imperial service for twelve years and was a good soldier. He was a son of Admiral Hockin of the British navy, and was thirty-seven years of age.

Dr. Stewart, who had been sent for when Allan was wounded, arrived during the afternoon. With him from Duck Lake came Postmaster Ernest Grundy and Messrs. Pozer, Davidson, Bell and Cook. At 6 o'clock it was decided to rush the bluff. The reason for this was that it was feared the Indians might make their escape in the darkness, the number of men being insufficient to guard it properly. The bluff is a hundred and fifty yards long by fifty wide at its greatest dimensions, composed of poplars, with a thick undergrowth of twisted gray willows, very difficult to penetrate. Near the western end the Indians had dug a pit with a butcher knife. It was oval in shape, about five feet long and four in depth.

The attacking party consisted of seven men and was led by Corporal Hockin. He had two policemen under him and four civilians, including Grundy, Cook and Davidson. The police,

Grundy and Cook entered the bluff at the western end and charged through it, firing as they went, without discovering the pit or provoking a response from the Indians. Then they faced about and came back on the other side.

The Indians lay perfectly still, reserving their fire until the white men were close upon them. Then three shots came in quick succession and Constable Kerr went down mortally wounded. Immediately after Grundy fell, killed. Hockin kept on, until stopped a moment later by a shot in the stomach. Constable Hume pluckily stayed by his corporal and dragged him out to a small open glade at the farther end of the bluff. Meanwhile the remainder of the whites kept the Indians engaged and in their pit, but they were unable to recover the bodies of Grundy and Kerr.

Louis Marion watched the fight from the top of the grassy slope on which, like an island, the bluff lay. A policeman (I could not learn his name) rushed up and told him that Hockin was shot. He asked for the loan of Marion's buckboard to carry him out of range.

Marion told the constable to jump in and drove down to the glade where the wounded man lay, with the faithful Hume keeping guard over him. It was an ugly spot, surrounded on three sides by the bluff, and Marion expected momentarily to hear the bullets of his desperate charges whistling about his ears. Poor Hockin was deathly pale and did not appear to suffer much. He was evidently dying and only in part conscious.

"I'm afraid he'll never stand the jolting of the buckboard," said Hume. "If you'll go back and get some blankets, we'll carry him up. I'll stay here."

Marion drove back up the slope with the other policeman and Dr. Stewart came to them, asking where Hockin was to be found. Marion gave him the buckboard and Stewart drove down to Hockin with Davidson and the policeman. Marion would have returned also but for the protests of his young son.

"You have already risked your life once," said the boy, "and you have a big family. Let some of the others go."

Hockin was placed on the rear of the buckboard with his back against the seat, on which Davidson knelt and held his shoulders. The policeman held Hockin's legs and Hume walked behind with his revolver to cover the retreat. Dr. Stewart led the horse. They had got only a few paces from the bluff when the Indians opened fire. One shot took a spoke out of the buckboard; another tipped Davidson's heel. Hume emptied his six shooter into the bluff and the Indians were driven back. The party at length got safely out of range.

Inspector Wilson arrived from the Lizard Hills—he discovered there was nothing for him to do there. The bluff was surrounded. Nobody slept. Poor Hockin lived only three hours. A big campfire burned at the top of the slope. Those not on duty lay about it. Now and then a bullet whistled over their heads in the darkness.

Almighty Voice was striving to satisfy his ambition to be great, and he and his companions sang songs weird and wild—songs such as no white man ever heard unless he has lived in their tents with the copper men—and shouted cries of defiance.

Next afternoon (Saturday) Superintendent Gagnon of the Mounted Police arrived with more men and a seven-pounder cannon from Prince Albert. With him came a party of some fifteen volunteers under James MacKay (later Mr. Justice MacKay of the Saskatchewan supreme court). The gun was posted on a ridge to the west and the bluff shelled.

At about 11 o'clock the same night Assistant Commissioner McIllree of the Mounted Police arrived from Regina with a nine-pounder cannon and twenty-five more men. By this time there were on the ground close to a hundred men and two cannon. It began to look unpromising for Almighty Voice's ambition.

It was dawn on the morning of May 26, 1897, and the angel of peace seemed to brood over all the virgin loveliness of the Saskatchewan.

But suddenly the roar of cannon broke the Sabbath stillness. Shrapnel, grape and cannister rained upon the little island of poplars in the smiling valley, plowing broad furrows through it, while the earth shook with the thunder of bursting shells. The outlook must have seemed very dispiriting to poor Almighty Voice and his companion, huddled in their little pit. I say companion, because one was dead, though the besiegers did not know this at the time.

Sounding Sky's wife sat on a hill and watched the engines of destruction trained upon the bluff. Who shall picture the feelings in the red woman's heart as their appalling discharges smote upon her ear? For after all, even if he had been wilful and bad, he was at least desperately brave, and he was her son. Now and then the defiant spit of an Indian rifle—like a firecracker in comparison—answered.

"I see you are prepared certainly to kill my son," she said to a passing police officer. "But I hope he will take some more with him, yet, when he goes!"

And so they sent the old woman back to her reserve. At 7 o'clock the firing ceased. At 9 it began again and continued for an hour. A council of war was held. Shovels, mattocks and grub hoes were sent for to Prince Albert. They would dig the hostiles out—approached by entrenchments. The volunteers asked to be allowed to rush the bluff again but this request the assistant commissioner refused for a moment to entertain.

"Enough lives have been lost already," he said.

At 2 o'clock the demand was renewed. Delay was growing irksome and all about the bluff was silent as the grave.

This time their request was granted. Led by James MacKay and William Drain, and accompanied by the police under Inspectors Wilson and McDonnell, they rushed, firing, upon the bluff.

They might have spared their ammunition. The Indians were all dead.

Almighty Voice and his Saulteaux cousin lay in the pit, the leader undermost, showing that he had been killed first. His skull had been smashed by a piece of shell and his thigh broken. On his ankle was a wound several days old—Sergeant Raven's shot. He wore part of Grundy's clothing.

The Saulteaux was killed by a fragment of shell. Dublin had been killed by a ball in the forehead—presumably fired by Almighty Voice. It is thought he had attempted to desert his companions. He was found in the edge of the bush behind where Hockin had lain before being removed from the bluff. He had been dead for many hours and was cold and stiff. He was dressed in Constable Kerr's tunic and breeches, and wore the policeman's gold ring upon his left hand.

The bodies of Kerr and Grundy were found where they had fallen. The former's head had been battered with a gun, which leads to the conclusion that he had not at once died of the bullet wound. The Indians had, of course, secured the guns and revolver of the dead men, but all except their pistol ammunition had been expended.

They had peeled the poplars surrounding their pit and chewed the bark—they must have suffered terribly from hunger and thirst. A crutch found seventy-five yards from the bluff and the trail left in the grass as he crept back, showed that Almighty Voice had made an effort to escape during the night after being wounded by Raven. Finding the bluff surrounded, he had been obliged to retreat to his cover again.

Thus ended Almighty Voice's war. Summed up, it accounted for the deaths of four white men and the wounding of three others, and closed with the deaths of Almighty Voice—who was little more than a boy himself—and his two reckless boy companions.

With it ended, too, the ambition of Almighty Voice, exactly where the ambitions of other men, sooner or later, end—in a hole.

I went with Louis Marion one day a good many years ago to Almighty Voice's Bluff. I looked into the little oval pit and found myself wondering how ever the three boys had managed to find cover at once in such a tiny burrow. I saw the peeled and shattered trees about it and walked round that small thicket island on the broad brown slope, while Marion pointed out where Hockin lay, where the crutch was found, and explained the details of the fight. Other particulars were furnished me by Dr. Stewart, for years the conscientious and skillful friend and medical attendant upon the Indians of Duck Lake agency, who took a prominent part in the affair and who knew Almighty Voice well.

Sounding Sky still lived on One Arrow's reserve. I saw the wife and sister of Almighty Voice, and his little son, whom he never saw. They never spoke of Almighty Voice then.

The Tale of a Shirt
or
The Adventures of an Indian Trader

Thus departed Hiawatha
To the land of the Dakotahs,
To the land of handsome women.

Picture to yourself a lonely, grass-grown cart trail, which seems to make for nowhere especially, but twists and winds and curves over prairies, through and around poplar and willow bluffs, miry alkali swamps and sedge-girt lakes, up and down steep, slippery hills and in and out of other impossible holes and places, with a plain disregard for the entirely modern idea of annihilating space. Note also a raw, wet afternoon—one of those cheerless, foreboding days in the early fall, when the mind of the youngster "roughing it" amid the wild scenes and dangers of life in the far West, who happens to be plodding slowly and dispiritedly through slush and mud, against rain and sleet, over such a trail, turns longingly and sadly—while perchance (shall I say it?) a salt drop mingles with the melting snow upon his cheek—to thoughts and memories of the cosy sitting room, the ruddy hearth and the kind, loving and beloved faces, warm hearts and fading eyes—the faint, broken "good-bye, God bless you, my boy!" of the "old folks at home."

It was on such a day, and under such conditions, toward the end of October, 1882, that, had you been near enough, you might have seen three solitary, dejected-looking human objects, a pair of horses and a loaded wagon on a trading expedition, creeping along the trail which leads eventually to the Cree and Assiniboine Indian reserves situated in the Eagle Hills, on the border of the Great Plains.

Reprinted from Waverley Magazine, *Boston, October 6, 1894.*

The first to observe of the trio composing the human part of the outfit was a tall, athletically built young settler of Irish extraction named Turner. The second was a little hunchbacked Nez Perce Indian called Jack—our interpreter, and the third was myself, whom you may designate the trader or the youngster, just as you choose.

It was the season of annuity payment to these Indians, who receive annually from the government a sum aggregating several thousands of dollars.

We arrived, in time, at the Cree reserve. Here we rented from an Indian one side of his house, divided off by an improvised counter of rough boards, behind which we stored our goods. This house, after the fashion of Indian dwellings in general, consisted only of a single room. In one corner was the open mud fireplace; in another the rude couch of the owner. Seating accommodation other than the bed and floor was manifestly regarded as superfluous; there was none.

During the afternoon the payments were complete and a number of the Indians had gathered at our trading post, among them *Peeaychew*, a man who, since the payments of last year, had "thrown away" (divorce is a very simple process amongst Indians) his wife with her children, and taken another.

The head of the family is paid for the whole. But *Peeaychew* had discarded his former mate; she was now the head of her own family. The agent was ignorant, however, at the moment of the change in the domestic position of the savage Lothario, and paid him, as before, for the companion and pledges of his first love.

Soon after, Mrs. *Peeaychew* No. 1 entered a complaint. Her former husband declined to part with any of the "shoonjaw."

"Hand her the pay of herself and children," ordered the agent. "You have no right to it."

Peeaychew only shook his head obstinately, and refused to obey.

"Oh, very well," said Mr. Reed. "But I shall take steps—sooner than you think—to recover the money." And he drove off.

Within fifteen minutes after he passed our door Colonel Herchmer drew up in a buckboard before it, accompanied by a sergeant and Mr. Reed's halfbreed interpreter, Josie. He entered, nodded, spoke a pleasant good-day to Turner and myself, and turning to Josie asked, pointing to the owner of the dwelling,

"Is that the man?"

"No," replied Josie. "That's him there—sitting on the bed."

"We'll soon fix him," remarked the colonel, and quickly crossing the room he said to *Peeaychew*,

"Hold out your hand."

A sickly pallor was showing beneath the sallow skin of the Indian. He did as he was ordered mechanically; an iron snapped upon his wrist, and retaining his grasp upon the other end of the shackle, the colonel, observing jocularly that it would puzzle them to understand how swiftly the white man's justice trod on the heels of wrong-doing, backed out of the house, drawing his prisoner after him. Arrived at the buckboard, the sergeant quickly attached a pair of heavy shackles to *Peeaychew's* ankles, he was lifted onto the rear part and the party spun rapidly away.

There is no such thing as rousing an Indian from a quiescent mood to a condition of immediate activity. He requires time to think before he can command his resources. The unexpected puts him in a panic; he is helpless, unnerved. And so quietly and adroitly had the arrest been effected that *Peeaychew's* fellow tribesmen sat motionless, silent, while he was being carried off "in durance vile." Then, as the buckboard rattled away through the bluffs along the trail in the distance, came the reaction. The women screamed and shouted in shrill voices, the daughters of the captive wept, the dogs howled, men ran about whooping and looking for their guns—a peaceful landscape for a nightmare.

"Say," ejaculated Turner, after taking in the run of events for awhile. "Things are beginnin' to look pretty lively. I hope they won't take it into their heads to try to gather an Injun revenge."

"I hope not," I rejoined very heartily.

"Indian revenge" is not white man's revenge. It is by no means essential that it should be inflicted upon the person whom he regards as the principal offender. If he be not available, a father, mother, brother or sister, will answer almost if not quite as well, and so on down through the widening grades of blood relationship. After that, one of the same nationality: then of the same race. To hamstring a horse or kill a dog will do in an extremity. It is hard to stick him. However, we did not suffer, and the next morning we rolled the trail for the Assiniboine Reserve.

On the Assiniboine Reserve were four head chiefs—Mosquito, Right-and-Left, Lean Man and Grizzly Bear's Head—with a village for the following of each. We secured a new log house, as yet doorless, in Lean Man's town, partitioning off a corner with our counter of rough boards.

Just as we completed the arrangement of our stock behind the counter, my patron, (I'm afraid I can't call him saint) Lean Man, came round to pay his respects. His title was not a misnomer. For a cursory view of him it will suffice to add that he was tall, had rather small eyes, very keen and bright, a low, smooth voice, and a deliberate and somewhat dignified air.

The incident which follows has really nothing to do with this story. Yet it serves to show why I was prepared to put up with perhaps more from Lean Man than most other Indians.

Stanley Simpson was a clerk in the Hudson's Bay Company's store at Battleford. One evening two Cree women came in and bought some vermilion. They opened the package, spilling part of the paint. Then there was not enough left to please them, and they asked Simpson to take it back. He refused, and they went out.

Lean Man came in a moment after. He had the vermilion in his hand. The women were not of his band; not even of his tribe.

"I want you to take this paint back and return the money," said he.

Simpson was writing at a desk behind the counter. He glanced up at the Indian and smiled.

"Hallo, Don Quixote the Second," he said in English. Then he said in Indian, "I have already refused to do that. Look after your own affairs, Lean Man."

"I never ask a man to do a thing oftener than three times," retorted the chief. Then, when he had repeated his demand twice, he drew a scalping knife from his belt and vaulted over the counter.

On the desk before Simpson lay a heavy ebony ruler. He watched the Indian covertly as he approached; he had an eye, also, on the ruler. Catching it up when the chief had come within reach, he brought it down (he was strong, too, was Simpson), right across his outstretched forearm.

The knife dropped at his feet; Lean Man then leaped back over the counter and ran out of the shop.

Now you will understand why I was inclined to be more than ordinarily deferential toward this particular Indian. I was upon his own exclusive territory, among perhaps as treacherous a tribe as may be found in the West. "Cut-Throat," an Indian of another nation designates the Assiniboine in the sign language, drawing his finger across his own windpipe. The action is a suggestive one, and the title fits him.

I offered no objection, therefore, when Lean Man salaamed low on the outside of our temporary counter and straightened himself up, smiling blandly, on the inside. With an emphasizing downward shake of his hand and much apparent warmth of manner, I invited him to a seat upon the most elegant vacant box that our establishment afforded, and presented him with a pound of tea, a plug of tobacco, and a package of sugar. He seemed pleased with the attention shown him, which he acknowledged by remarking in his soft, melodious accents, "Good heart," with the appropriate movement of his hand expressive of the same sentiment in the language of signs. I felt that it lent an air of tone to our party to be thus the object of a princely recognition.

Lean Man smoked reflectively for a time. He did not discuss the weather and those other ever fruitful and charming topics of civilized life. Then he picked up an undershirt—price one dollar and twenty-five cents—and said he thought he would take it. The payments had not yet begun; he would call and pay for it later. Of course, I was pleased. He then threw off his blanket, which was all the clothing he wore just at the time, above his waist, and pulled the garment on over his head.

It may be observed that an undershirt is not necessarily such in the view of the sagacious red man. A single shirt, from motives either of economy or choice—or both—usually supplies the purpose of both an outer and an inner one, regardless of the design of the maker as to how it was to be worn. Should he be the fortunate possessor of two, and feel disposed at any time to don them both, he is as likely as not to reverse the established order of arrangement by putting the outside one next his person, and the undershirt, the proper place of which has been thus usurped over it.

"The Princess Lean Man and suite"—those "handsome Dakotah maidens" of Longfellow! What a vision of rounded litheness, of sapling grace—of fair-dark beauty! Of lashes sweeping and eyes soft as a doe's—for all so jet and sparkling! They stood about in groups, casting shy furtive glances at us and the finery scattered round. And then, after they had received the gum for which they pleaded, the dazzle of ivory, the running fire of holiday torpedoes!

But, back to our story!

Late in the afternoon I walked up from our trading post to Right-and-Left's house. Here I found the agent, hemmed in at the farther end by the body of the chief warriors of the different bands, seated at a small table with his clerk—and interpreter as well—poor, brave, faithful Tom Quinn, killed three years later when these Indians took the warpath against the whites. Behind them stood three troopers, with their clean scarlet tunics and yellow-banded forage caps, a belt of shining cartridges and heavy navy revolver at the waist of each.

Chief Grizzly Bear's Head was speaking—a superb specimen of the typical warrior of the Dakotahs. Tall and stalwart, fierce in mien and deportment, his features strong, massive, and stamped with expressive lines, his cheek bones high, lips thin and cruel looking, and jaw heavy and full of power. About his shoulders hung his long, plaited black hair, matted and interwoven, wound with steel and copper wire; above the war-lock floated a glossy, jet-tipped plume from the tail of an eagle. One over another, from the edges of his ears, depended brass rings, two or three inches in diameter. If his name was not made for him, he was made for his name.

I shall not attempt to interpret his speech. Enough to say that from the surge of *"How! How!"* which broke forth at the close of each flowing period from a hundred bronze throats, it was evident that he embodied the sentiment of the whole dark assembly. Ringing, declamatory, fell his words—impassioned his gestures; he was savage oratorical art personified.

"The Dakotahs wanted beef before they would consent to take their treaty money!"

"It is not in the treaty stipulations," remonstrated the agent.

Whether the "bone of contention"—the unfatted calf, fifteen hands high, with thirteen crinkles in his horns, went to the Indians, or whether the government kept it to pull a plow for them another spring, I do not know; for, the sun now blazing a glorious good evening to everything and everybody, I very soon returned to our post.

During the night a pair of wolfish dogs appropriated the cellar where we had thrown some partially spoiled hams. They could not get out again without help; the hole was too deep. If they did not literally "make Rome howl," faint echoes of their notes must at least have reached Spain. We could not sleep, so we got up and peered into the cellar in the dark. A medley of red eyes and vicious snaps and snarls greeted us.

"Perhaps we'd better not disturb these timid creatures," I suggested.

No dissenting voice.

"Carried unanimous," declared Turner. "We will lave thim to their innocent divarshun till the owner hooks thim out in the mornin'."

Which we did.

Next day the payments began, and I then had quite sufficient to occupy my attention at my place of business.

An Indian when he commences to buy can't do it fast enough. He may ponder and drop from one trader's post into another's, and on to the next and back again; ask prices and beg and conduct himself otherwise in such a manner as seems to the expectant trader extremely perverse, slow and altogether unnecessary; but suddenly he makes up his mind. Out comes his roll of crisp new bills (treaty money), and blankets, flour, paint, bacon, earrings, sugar, tea and thread are fairly fired at him; a broadside of powder, shot, caps, gunflints, nails, knives, scissors, beads and tin cups rakes his starboard quarter; at his head fly hats, feathers, candy, tobacco, scarlet stroud (course blanket), red cotton handkerchiefs and gum—until the roll has transferred itself from his hand to the trader's pocket. When a place is full and a dozen fists are thrusting crackling notes into one's face at once, it may be imagined that, as they say in the West, in language more forcible than elegant, it keeps the trader "humping."

After three days among the Assiniboines we returned to town, our pockets bulging with one dollar notes.

"Ah yes—the shirt. Back to the story."

Before we left, Lean Man paid me another visit. His manner was, if possible, even more deliberate, solemn and impressive than customary. He dodged gracefully under the counter again and helped himself to a seat, where he smoked in silence for some time.

"White man," he said at length in his dulcet tones, "I have decided after much thought that I do not want your shirt. The quality is not quite what I supposed it to be. I will therefore return it to you."

He rose and placidly drew it over his head. He had worn it three days.

"But," said I, holding it off at a respectful distance on the point of one finger, "this is not my shirt."

"It is the same which you gave unto me," replied Lean Man, reassuringly.

A more critical examination showed that he spoke the truth. I found the price mark in my own figures; there was no disputing it. But the shirt he had bought from me was white, whereas this one was, well, not white.

"Take it for a dollar," said I, presenting it to him with an air of reckless generosity, as though offering a great bargain.

"No, white man," he answered, "though it is a nice shirt and cheap, I must buy chewing gum for my little grandson, who will cry else; and therefore I cannot take it."

I turned and threw it at the Nez Perce. He appreciated the favour. Doubtless the fact that it had been worn by the redoubtable redskin enhanced its value in his eyes. He probably imagined it would be a shirt of mail—impervious to bullets.

Once again their customs stood revealed. This warlike people firmly believed that a survivor of many battles and all that he used, wore or owned is touched with magic and carries with it the power to protect the one who falls heir to it.

It was no dirty shirt I gave to the Nez Perce—it was good medicine!

A Night in the Dakotah Camp

Looking back at those early trading days in the 1880s there stand out incidents from which we were fortunate to escape with all the hairs on our heads, Turner, the Nez Perce and myself. Our reception at the Assiniboine Reserve was such a one.

By evening of that chill October day, the gala time of the improvident Stoney's year—his hour of wealth—was past; the annuities had all been paid—and spent again. But the pockets of his pale-skinned brother were in a distressing state of gorge, trade had been brisk.

"Come up to the shack and have a dance tonight; I'll supply the refreshments," I said.

I wanted to show that I could appreciate their friendship and new Dominion bills; especially the bills. I am a little doubtful though. I was among as thievish and cut-throat a bunch of rascals as one might stumble into anywhere, even in the West, on their own exclusive territory. Their goodwill was worth considering on that score at least.

Speaking of cut-throats, a word, by way of interjection, about sign language: Two braves meet. They are of different tribes, ignorant of one another's tongue. One pushes the forefinger of his right hand over his lip, he is a Nez Perce, or pierced nose; the other draws the same finger across his throat, he is a Dakotah, or Stoney, or a cut-throat.

About eight o'clock they arrived—two or three minor chiefs and thirty or forty of the younger bucks. To describe here their naked limbs, the gorgeousness of their paints, plumes, weapons and general warlike appearance, or the dance itself, would be to encroach on unceded ground.

Reprinted from Waverley Magazine, *Boston, December 1, 1894.*

It was growing late, between eleven and twelve, I think. The large kettle of tea had vanished, the dancers seemed tired, and it looked as if they would soon take their leave. Turner and I leaned over the counter facing the doorway, a tin of melted fat in which flared a bit of calico between us, while the Nez Perce sat on the end of the counter beside the open mud chimney, his back against the log wall, and his hands clasped before his knees.

Among the dancers was an Indian with whom I had had some trouble during the summer—an impudent, lazy rascal with a large, Roman nose and several big brass rings jingling in his ears—half Stoney, half Cree. This man now suddenly arose and advancing to the counter placed his hand on Turner's chest, passing some remark meanwhile to the others which I did not understand. He then turned to me and repeated the action.

Stowed snugly away in the inner breast pocket of my coat was a leather wallet containing our cash receipts, which from its bulk, owing to the number of notes it held, showed plainly on the outside. As his hand fell upon this, he bent forward and with a quick puff extinguished the light. I drew back on the instant and made a pass at him with my right hand, which in the murky gloom (the fire had burned low) he avoided, relinquishing, however, at the same time, his hold upon the pocket book.

"What shall we do, Bill?" I said in a low tone to Turner.

"Light the dip again," he replied. "I reckon they're on the steal."

I struck a match, but before I could touch it to the cotton the menacing savage blew it out. Then another and another.

"It's not worth while our getting hostile, Bill, I guess," I was trying all I knew how to keep cool, "there's too many of them. Even with the aid of our pistols, if it came to that, we'd stand mighty little show of leaving here."

"Besides, it wouldn't do at all," rejoined Turner. "Why, if blood flowed through us they'd massacre every white man and helpless woman and young 'un in the country, and raid Battleford inside of twenty-four hours. Still, we've got to protect ourselves, that's all, if they mean mischief. If they must have lead," he went on, his voice rising with his quick Irish blood, "they will get it, let the consequences be what they may."

I lifted the tin off the boards, stepped back a couple of paces, and lighted it. The aggressor still stood facing us, a saucy, sneering smile on his lips, his hand upon a knife at his belt, speaking in rapid, almost inaudible tones to the others, who stood or shifted uneasily about, their eyes burning with subdued excitement, some toying nervously with the locks of their guns.

Of the minor chiefs one was a tall, powerful warrior whom I had assisted at different times during the previous winter when he was starving about town. He had kept his seat, leaning back against the chimney while all this was going on, saying nothing.

Gratitude or friendship is a hard quality to depend too strongly upon in an Indian; I had discovered that from experience. However, it was worth a trial. Turning to the Nez Perce I said,

"Jack, tell *Ta-tonka Nompa* that I am surprised that he allows the young men to behave as they are doing. I thought he was my friend. I have helped him more than once, as he well knows, when he was grateful to me for food, and I did not think his face would be turned from me now. This man who blew the light out is my enemy and would do me harm. Tell him, Jack—tell *Ta-tonka Nompa* things look bad—very bad. Will he let this go further? It will only make trouble between us all."

Slowly the chief rose. He stood nearly a head over any of the others—even the brazen belligerent opposite him. Then, stretching out his clenched fist toward the latter, he spoke very calmly and deliberately,

"I will break that eagle nose of yours—perhaps will kill you—if you further offend the white man, my brother here. He has shown a good heart toward you; and now, dog that you are, you try to anger him, that you may find excuse to create a row—to stab him in the dark and rob him. If you or any other wish to fight, strike—strike me! No? Then leave! Go, I say!" and he took a menacing step forward.

The unruly brave turned sulkily on his heel and, casting back at us over his shoulder a parting scowl of baffled rage and sullen hate, bounded with a long, ringing whoop of defiance into the sable woof of the night and disappeared, his fellows, like the legion of a peer of darkness, sweeping, with a chorus of yells, in his train.

Ta-tonka Nompa remained with us until daybreak, as surety against further annoyance, spinning many picturesque yarns of earlier, less peaceful days, for we did not care to seek our blankets. Our little hunchbacked Nez Perce, Jack, too, told how he got the white mark through his eyebrow.

We arrived in Battleford the same evening, not altogether sorry to have said a farewell "How" to our enterprising and lively friends, the Dakotahs, the Stoneys or the Cut-Throats.

The Shame of Many
Brave Feathers

That the civilized world quaked in its shoes at the thunders of
Waterloo was nothing to Many Brave Feathers. He did not care in
the least about the small Corsican. The truth was that he had
never heard of him or his fortunes. Had he met Napoleon and
learned of his prowess, he would doubtless have hailed him as a
worthy brother and, with a certain surprised contempt at his
diminutive proportions diluting his esteem, have given him the
chief place of honour (after his own) at the very first dog feast. As
matters stood, however, he had no one with whom he might share
his laurels.

Within his own primitive range he was as big a man as the
French Emperor; in stature he was very much bigger, and the
territory which he swayed was, perhaps, not greatly inferior in
area to that over which Bonaparte had extended his conquests.
Commencing on the east at the Red River, only when he came
close to the towering Rockies did he encounter a foe that disputed
his pretensions—the uncompromising Blackfoot. And who among
all his followers, whether of his own tribe, the Cree, or of their
allies, the Assiniboine and the Saulteaux, could boast of such feats
of sorcery, such daring on the war trail, of such invariable good
luck in midnight raids as could Many Brave Feathers? Why, his
name had become a synonym for success; they had even given
him a new one—"The One Who Wins." And what chief beside
himself could keep his warriors wondering days together when
things of high moment were on the wind; then suddenly transfix
them with a burst of impassioned eloquence, unfolding his plans
at the council he had called or by a dazzling coup?

"Great is *Kahmeesohetookeehewup!*" exclaimed the braves at such
times. "There is none like unto him!"

Reprinted from the New York Sun, *May 17, 1896.*

And the warrior chief, sitting apart in his gaudy leathern robe, with the firelight playing in his black eyes and on the grave painted face, crowned by a bunch of glorious eagle plumes, "with ravished ears," was wont, like Alexander, to

> Assume the god,
> Affect to nod,
> And seem to shake the spheres.

It was in the fall that Many Brave Feathers left the centre of his domain, Fort Ellice, at the head of the war party on this incursion into the Blackfoot country. The Cree were short of horses. The Blackfoot, when they were short of horses crossed the mountains and stole from the Nez Perce and the Kootanay: then the Cree in turn stole from them. Many Brave Feathers and his men brought plenty of lines, for they would surely get many ponies, they thought. They slept many times before they reached disputed ground. The conjuror set up his lodge and, with the seer's power, he told them that the enemy was close and that they must send out three spies.

At the council that night they selected them. One was *Ameequan*, The Spoon. Few of the warriors were so brave as was *Ameequan*. Another was Many Brave Feathers. The spies traveled several days; then they thought they saw signs. *Ameequan* told his companions to stay where they were until he came again, and went further in search of the enemy.

Many Brave Feathers saw the sun set six times while he had waited for *Ameequan:* then at the head of his war party he started for the point where he was to fall in with the main camp of his people on his return. His usual reckless courage seemed to have forsaken him—that doubtful fate of *Ameequan!* And the war party was not large.

Now *Ameequan*, when he parted from the other two, went on for some time. At length, about daybreak of a foggy morning, he heard the howl of a wolf. But *Ameequan* was not to be deceived; he was too good a plainsman for that.

"A Blackfoot scout," he whispered. He stopped and listened intently. "No answer? Then he is alone, too," and into his eyes came the hard glitter of resolve.

He went softly toward the sound. The heavy gray mist lay thick on the brown, withered grass of the treeless plains; it shut out all a few steps off. He stole forward like a lynx—warily, making no noise—until at last, sitting on a hill, just before him, was a man.

He dropped his gun and prepared to creep. Every time the unsuspecting Blackfoot howled, *Ameequan* shortened the space separating them. Now he was close upon him. With the rush of a grizzly he launched himself at the Blackfoot, winding him in his arms, and crushed him to the earth. Over and over they rolled. Their breath came in short, hard gasps, with low, strange oaths from between their clenched teeth. The good spirits helped *Ameequan*—he was stronger than the other. Now the Blackfoot was under. His knife still stuck in the sheath. *Ameequan* made a clutch for it, pulled, and flung it away on the prairie. Then he drew his own knife and held the point against his rival's throat.

"Yield, Blackfoot, whelp of a she wolf," he cried. "I have won!"

Sullenly the Blackfoot made the sign of submission, and *Ameequan* let him rise. He stood stolid, indifferent, waiting his vanquisher's further commands.

Ameequan took him to where he had left his gun and the lines he had brought for stealing horses. He tied his captive's hands behind him and made him walk before him for two days. They had nothing to eat all this time.

On the third day they saw buffalo. *Ameequan* bound the Blackfoot hand and foot, and left him lying on the prairie while he went and killed a fat cow. He brought his prisoner up to the dead animal, and they ate much. Then he loaded what meat was required on the captive, and they went on as before—*Ameequan* always trying, with the few words of Blackfoot he knew, aided by signs, to make him understand that he would not be killed. After three days more hard traveling, they at length approached the spot appointed for the rendezvous.

It was night. Blackness hung like the wing of a raven over plain and valley. It wrapped as a blanket the high, ragged range of hills in the midst of which lay the camp. The measured sound of the big drum blended with the shrill, weird chant of the drummers, and rolled away through the reverberating gloom till lost in faint echoes among the mountain fastnesses. It proclaimed to the startled wolf, the bear and the wapiti that a big war dance heralded the arrival of the war party. True, they had brought no horses, had accomplished nothing except leave one of their bravest (hairless, probably, and with the buzzards now feeding between his ribs) behind. And that, surely, was cause sufficient to celebrate, to boast of past bravery and of the harvest of revenge to be reaped after a while.

There was a lull in the dancing, and the boom of the drum: Many Brave Feathers had arisen to speak. They were all painted. Over his shoulder was flung his soft-tanned buffalo skin. Upon it in places were crimson spots, tokens of wounds received in many

a fierce encounter; there were other symbols, too, of horses he had
stolen, and of enemies whose scalps floated from his coup stick.
His chest and right arm were naked. The many plumes fastened in
his war plait nodded dignifiedly with each movement of his limbs
and body. On his left arm rested a bundle of dry poplar sticks; his
right hand held as a fan the dark, glossy wing of an eagle, which
he used in the gestures that embellished his speech and to point in
the direction of each successive exploit he related.

As each deed was told off, taking a stick from his arm, with a
step or two nearer the centre of the circle, he placed it upon the
fire. As stick after stick was added to the red, thirsty pile, the
adulatory *"How! How!"* burst from the surrounding ranks of his
seated warriors, emphasized by a volley like a salute of honour
from a line of musketry sounded upon the drum by the
drummers; the flames leaped up, higher, brighter, as though
exulting with them in his triumphs.

He had told an adventure for every stick but one. The fan he
had transferred to his left hand and he was indicating with the last
billet in his right the position of the Medicine Hat and recounting
his most noted achievement. They never wearied of that. It was a
tale of his younger days.

They were fighting the Blackfoot. One of the young men of the
Blackfoot wished to show himself braver than the others; he rode
like the whirlwind close down the Cree front, shooting his arrows
among them. Many Brave Feathers followed. The Blackfoot
turned toward his friends. Still the young Cree followed; he was
overhauling him. The faces of the enemy were in a row before
him when he caught his horse; their eyes were like fire, while
arrows were singing all around. He leaned forward with a great,
flashing buffalo knife in his hand. He struck him a backward
blow, just once, across the belly. There was nothing left but the
bone behind and the Blackfoot fell. Then Many Brave Feathers
galloped back.

Every neck was craning forward, every eye was fixed upon him,
every ear was intent not to lose a word; it was the deep stillness
before the breaker of applause. As he spoke the last sentence he
heard his name called aloud outside the dancing lodge, and he
paused in the act of placing the last stick upon the fire. It was
Ameequan's voice. It said:

"Kahmeeschetookeehewup! I have brought the man you all ran away
from! I wish to bring him into the tent!"

"I told him to bring him in, and I adopted the Blackfoot as my
son. But still I was ashamed," added Many Brave Feathers, when
he told the story in his garrulous old age.

Crafty Many Brave Feathers
(Fiction)

"*Kahmeeschetookeehewup*, will you ride a fine horse once?"

The Cree chief looked at the handsome black mare the chief factor was leading towards him; then he called one of his braves. "Bring my painted buffalo robe and my bow and feathered arrows," he said.

He mounted and rode back some way along the trail which stretched over the undulating prairie and on far to the south, where the buffalo fattened numberless on the rich grass. He would "run" the mare as though he were running buffalo; he would show these white men how Many Brave Feathers hunted!

He turned and gave her her head. On he came, like the hawk, shooting his arrows at the little poplars in the bluffs along the trail as he rode. A crowd had assembled to see the run; part were his own people, the others the staff of the Hudson's Bay Company at Fort Ellice.

He was riding very fast. As he neared the stockade he tried to pull the mare in. But she declined to be pulled in; she was just getting nicely going.

"*Ay-ay-yah!*" yelled the spectators, giving the war whoop as he shot past, and he kept on and circled the fort.

Now a bad thought came into his head; he would run away with the mare!

The chief factor's face did not entirely hide the feeling of chagrin with which he beheld his favourite beast vanish over a slope in the south under the sailing buffalo skin. Then he went to his quarters. The features of the other on-lookers wore a big general smile as he disappeared. The genial sun smiled broadly

Reprinted from Harper's Weekly, *New York, June 15, 1895, and June 27, 1896.*

too, in the summer sky; in fact, everything seemed smiling—except the chief factor.

"Well, if that ain't a good un!" remarked the clerk to the rest of the staff as they sauntered back.

Many Brave Feathers passed the night at Moose Mountain. This is only seventy-five miles from Fort Ellice, but then it was afternoon when he started. Next day he arrived at a camp of his own tribe and some Assiniboines on Broken Shell Creek in the buffalo country.

All that fall and winter he stayed out on the plains, running buffalo with the stolen horse, though he never lent her to anyone except his sweetheart, who used to ride her when they moved camp. In the spring, when the grass was green, the camp, with its store of robes and cured meat, journeyed toward Fort Ellice. Many Brave Feathers ordered one of his men to catch him three horses out of the band. He came to the fort riding the mare and leading the three other horses, and asked for the chief factor. He had had the mare seven moons, but she had been well cared for and was fat.

"Ah-ha, *Mistahuse*, you speak true. The mare is very fast," he said, as he put the lines of the four horses into the chief factor's hand.

"Blamed if I wouldn't like some aboriginal Ceasar to borrow my doggoned pinto cayuse for six months on the same terms!" exclaimed the clerk. He thought the old man had the best of it after all.

He Decides to Have a Government School

"I have thought much of your talk last year and in the years before, Son of the Great White Mother," said Many Brave Feathers, after smoking reflectively for a time. "Many times it has come into my head. I wish to please the Great White Mother; I will have the school."

The Inspector of Indian Agencies drew himself up with dignity. He wore a frock coat, gloves, and a tall hat.

"The Great White Mother will be exceedingly pleased, Many Brave Feathers," he said. "She will be glad—glad to learn that her son Many Brave Feathers, the wise and strong, chief of the great Plains Cree nation, has come to see the benefits which will accrue to the children of his people from the white man's education. They will be enabled, by the study of the industrial and economic arts and of the usages of civilized society, to clothe and support themselves like us, as becomes good citizens of our fair

Dominion. I am proud to be the bearer of your message to the Great Mother."

The Cree chief threw the soiled and tattered white blanket back over his shoulder, with a gesture of slight impatience.

"Much talk with big words is very good sometimes when there are plenty to hear, though they do not know the Great White Mother is very good to her poor red children, and her palefaced sons fill our ears with a pleasant sound when they speak, though we do not understand. But wait: big words are not so good for me as little, nor much talk; yet I have more to say. The Great White Mother will let me name the one who shall show my children what they should know."

"It is well," replied the Inspector. "You will of course choose one who is filled with learning. Meanwhile I shall secure a house temporarily in which to hold the school, and shall send you books, maps, and everything necessary. At noon each day the children attending will be fed by the teacher—biscuits and rice."

"And will the teacher be fed too?" asked the chief.

"What's he say?" asked the Inspector of the interpreter.

"She says: 'The teacher, him, will she get grub too?' answered the halfbreed, promptly, with the easy confidence bred of conscious mastery of the intricacies of the tongue *Anglais.*

"No; he will have to feed himself; but the good White Mother will pay him twenty-five dollars each month for teaching the school."

"But he will have charge of the biscuits and the rice?"

"Yes."

"And the first twenty-five dollars—will she pay it now?"

"No; at the end of the month."

"It is good. Tomorrow morning the Son of the Great White Mother will come again to my tent. The teacher will be, the children will be, and the school shall begin. He may send the biscuits and the rice, but he need not bring books; I have all that is wanted, and a map."

This hit the Inspector as a somewhat novel arrangement, but he said nothing. Things sometimes took on unaccustomed aspects in these Indian negotiations, and one had to be diplomatic. Getting in the thin edge of the wedge was the great point. All would be resolved to order in time.

At ten o'clock next day the Inspector, with his staff, alighted before the door of Many Brave Feathers's lodge and the chief solemnly motioned him to a seat opposite himself on the floor inside. Half a dozen copper-hided little ones looked at him awfully out of steely eyes, but he saw no one else.

"The teacher—he has not yet arrived, Many Brave Feathers?" said the Inspector.

"He is here," returned the chief, tapping his chest with his right-hand forefinger. "*I* am the teacher. Children," he continued, turning to the youthful group, "the lesson will now commence."

The Inspector's secretary, the Commandant of the Mounted Police, the Indian Agent, and the Chief Factor of the Hudson's Bay Company were taking covert glances at the Inspector, with faint suggestions of amusement discernible in the lines about their mouths and eyes. The Inspector's face, on the contrary, betrayed no such feelings, but was, in fact, set in lines of severe rigidity. His tall hat looked particularly tall and straight. As many of the warriors as could be seen through the open doorway and under the rolled-up tent curtain wore comprehensive grins.

The chief picked up a long, heavy hunting knife and indicating the floor with a sweep of his arm, resumed:

"This is my map—a little bit of the big country which you will see when you go outside in two smokes to play with the horses and practise with your bows and arrows."

He sunk the knife deep in the ground, turned up a handful of soil, and went on:

"Children, this is your father and your mother. You spring from this; from this the grass grows when the snow melts and the rain falls. The buffalo eat the grass—you eat the buffalo. So you live, because your father and your mother feed you; and when you die you go to earth again, and again the grass grows over you.

"Children, the school is over for today. Remember what I have told you. Running Antelope, is the rice cooked? Running Antelope hobbled up to the kettle and peered into it. Yes, the rice was cooked.

"Then," concluded Many Brave Feathers, "I will eat some to see that it is good, and I will also eat cakes of the hard flour which the kind Great White Mother sends, to know that they are not bad and will not harm our little ones. When you have eaten plenty, children, you will go outside and see more of my big country, of which I showed you a little on the map. Then you will be strong and not afraid to ride the saddleless horses which are not yet well broken, nor to leave the camp to kill rabbits with your bows and arrows.

"And when the Great White Mother gives me the twenty-five dollars at the end of the moon, we will have a big war dance and you shall come and taste white dog to make you strong hearts, and hear how your fathers won their Blackfoot scalps.

"*How! how!* Son of the Great White Mother and her Message Bearer, I salute you!"

It was some years after the formal opening by Many Brave Feathers of his school before a regularly appointed institution of the government order was established upon his reserve.

Notes to Introduction

1. Canon Bleasdell served his church in Trenton about forty years. When he died he was buried under the altar of St. George's church.
2. Alexander Macdonald, then a small jobber, later became the millionaire proprietor of Macdonald's Consolidated.
3. Letter of recommendation in the Cameron Papers. These papers are in possession of the Cameron heirs.
4. The letter was discovered eighty-three years later in the Wister Papers, Manuscript Division, Library of Congress, Washington, D.C.
5. Cameron had three sisters and a brother. By this time, the oldest sister, Isabelle, was Lady Bourinot, wife of Sir John Bourinot, historian and longtime Chief Clerk of the House of Commons. Second sister, Agnes, apparently went west with her mother when Cameron was a civil servant after the 1885 Rebellion. Possibly at the Regina NWMP Depot she met Inspector Joseph Howe, whom she married. He became a major, second in command of the Canadian Mounted Rifles in the Boer War, 1900, and then Commanding Officer of the NWMP post of Macleod. He died there in 1902. Cameron's youngest sister, Maude, married Col. J. A. Macdonnell, later a railway developer in Vancouver, B.C. Cameron's younger brother, Charles, went west and met Bleasdell after his release from captivity. Charles eventually became a sailor, plying the Pacific coast to the Yukon, Washington coastal waters, and the Columbia and Kootenay river systems.
6. *The Bulletin*, Brooks, July 20, 1961. Article by Leonard D. Nesbitt.
7. Letter from Howard A. Kennedy, quoted in promotional material in the Cameron Papers.
8. Letter, W. B. Cameron to Douglas Cameron, Dec. 24, 1950. Cameron Papers.
9. Douglas Cameron married Elsie Noreen Stewart-Clough, daughter of Brig.-Gen. J. R. Stewart-Clough, of Vancouver, early in the Second World War. After war service, Douglas became an advertising

executive in Montreal. In 1938 he also was a top seeded member of Canada's Davis Cup tennis team, competing internationally. Owen Cameron married Jessie Muir Chapman, daughter of a North Vancouver school board official. In his young years Owen was a runner, boxer, and was a boomer in the B.C. lumbering industry.

10. Cameron Papers.

11. In 1931, Cameron was in Vancouver for a time, editing *Scarlet and Gold* but payment for the work was not enough to provide a living. There also are indications that he may have worked as telegraph editor at one of Vancouver's daily newspapers.

12. Letters, Annett to Cameron, Oct. 15, 1945, and Feb. 3, 1946. Cameron Papers.

13. Letters, Annett to Cameron, including July 19, Sept. 23, Oct. 24, Nov. 20, 28, 1945; May 26, Nov. 7, 1946; Jan. 30, 1947; and March 22, 1948. Cameron Papers.

14. Cameron, writing to "Nosiseem," June 23, 1947. Cameron Papers.

15. Undated clipping, ca.1944, in the Cameron Papers.

16. Several such meetings took place between Cameron and the writer at the Editorial offices of the Western Producer, Saskatoon, in 1950 and 1951.

17. Saskatoon *Star-Phoenix*, Oct. 22, 1947.

18. Letter, Cameron to Luxton, Banff, Alta., April 5, 1948.

19. Craig had been a pioneer businessman at Vermilion, Alta., and knew Cameron from 1905 onward.

20. Cameron Papers.

21. Most details of Cameron's last days and funeral were drawn from a letter from Douglas to Owen, March 8, 1951. Douglas, the only family member present at the burial, paid the expenses. Cameron Papers.

22. Letter, Wister to Cameron, July 5, 1899. Cameron Papers.

23. Notes taken by W. P. Bate at the Saskatchewan Historical Society meeting. Morton Papers, University of Saskatchewan Library, Saskatoon.

24. See Stuart Hughes, *The Frog Lake Massacre*, Toronto: McClelland and Stewart, 1976.

Index

Some Indians appear under Indian names, others under English or French names. Where it is clear that an Indian is referred to, that name appears as a subentry under the comprehensive "Indians" heading. If not clear, then it appears in the general alphabetical index. Illustrations are indicated by page numbers set in bold face type.

About the Editor

R. H. "Rusty" Macdonald began his career in journalism as a reporter for the *Regina Leader Post*. In 1949 he joined the staff of *The Western Producer* and was later appointed executive editor, a position he held until his retirement in 1977.

It was while he was acting as executive editor that he encountered William Bleasdell Cameron. Macdonald bought articles from Cameron for the newspaper and became interested in Cameron's experiences as an "eyewitness" to the early history of the West. After Macdonald retired, he began to look for Cameron's heirs, hoping to republish his early works. The search led eventually to an old trunk, literally stuffed with manuscripts and articles, in the attic of Cameron's daughter-in-law.

Macdonald lives in Saskatoon with his wife, Doris, and works as a consulting journalist, author, and photographer. To date his books include three photographic works — *Four Seasons West, Saskatchewan Landscapes,* and *Alberta Landscapes,* with text by Grant MacEwan; a biography entitled *Grant MacEwan: No Ordinary Man; In a Manner of Speaking,* a toastmaster's guide based on his own experience as a reporter covering meetings and "the banquet beat"; and *The Best of Grant MacEwan,* which he edited.